negotiating licences for digital resources

negotiating licences for digital resources

Fiona Durrant

facet publishing

© Fiona Durrant 2006

Published by
Facet Publishing
7 Ridgmount Street
London WC1E 7AE
www.facetpublishing.co.uk

Facet Publishing is wholly owned by CILIP: the Chartered Institute of Library and Information Professionals.

Fiona Durrant has asserted her right under the Copyright, Designs and Patents Act, 1988 to be identified as author of this work.

First published 2006

British Library Cataloguing in Publication Data
A catalogue record for this book is available from the British Library.

ISBN-13: 978-1-85604-586-5
ISBN-10: 1-85604-586-2

Typeset in 11/15 pt University Old Style and Zurich Expanded by Facet Publishing.
Printed and made in Great Britain by MPG Books Ltd, Bodmin, Cornwall.

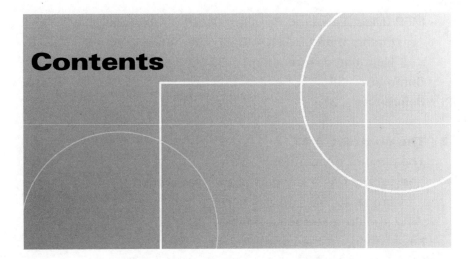

Contents

Acknowledgements

This book has been the result of experience in the workplace and the attempt to write down what worked and to learn from what did not work. I could not have written this book without all the people I meet and work with in my day-to-day career. However, I cannot make generalizations about the contributions made by past and present bosses, Alex Kleanthous and Jennifer Barrow, who have taught me so much. I must also mention my faithful work colleagues, especially Anne, Dunstan, Susanna and Andrew, who also use the products I negotiate for and help provide me with material for the all-important preparation phase of a negotiation. My regard for the work of Mike Taylor is also very evident in this book, being a trainer who presented his ideas in a very comprehensive and digestible manner, and he has kindly permitted me to use a couple of those ideas here.

I also would not have had reason to write this book if I had not been inspired by the quandaries that negotiation of an online subscription brings, so thanks also go to the representatives and publishers who make my working life so very interesting.

On a personal level thanks to my very supportive husband Mike, my mum Ann, and my angelic daughter Annie. Also to my Dad, who showed me from an early age that writing a book, having a career and being a parent was possible, without compromising on the love that was shared in the household. I started writing this book when Annie was only a few months old, and I could not have done it if I had not had the best support in the world and the most well behaved baby who so very much liked her sleep.

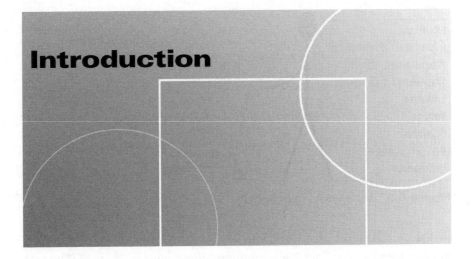

Introduction

Who is this book for?

Negotiating is something people do in everyday life. Authors negotiate with their publishers for extensions to deadlines, buyers of houses negotiate with the vendor or estate agent, employees negotiate with their employers about the terms of their engagement. Information, however, has its own quirks and relationships, which, when understood in depth, can lead to getting the best deal for both purchaser and vendor. This book will help information professionals in all sectors, and all jurisdictions, on how to get the best deal for their organization (see Figure 0.1). It can act as a reference tool for experienced negotiators or as a primer for those who have never before been involved in the process.

Online subscriptions range from e-journals to multi-modular databases, from proprietary content to collations of third-party materials. What these online resources have in common is that someone has to decide to buy them, actively purchase them, manage them and then use them. Sometimes these roles are not performed by the same person, but each role has a contribution to make in the negotiation process (see Table 0.1).

The key concepts behind the negotiation of online subscriptions have few sectoral or geographical borders. The tips and methods that will be found in the following chapters will aid any individual or team involved

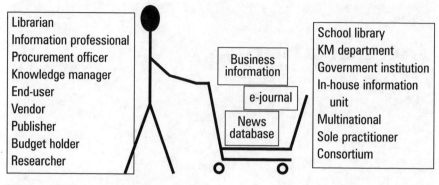

Figure 0.1 Varieties of negotiation

in the purchase of electronic media, ranging from the librarian and knowledge professional to procurement officers and publishers. The sole librarian will benefit as much as the head of a large department. It may be that a sole practitioner in a profession has to purchase online resources and to keep overheads as low as possible. This title will benefit them and those for whom they do work.

This book can be used by mentors to involve junior members of staff in the negotiation process, and it can be used by the users of the electronic products to ensure that they are providing useful feedback about the resources they are using to the person who is going to be doing the negotiation. The processes explained in this book can apply to individual contracts as well as multi-site international licences.

Contributors to the negotiation process on the purchaser's side are outlined in Table 0.1. In some small information units or for the sole practitioner it may be that one person plays all these roles.

What is negotiation?

When buying a house, most purchasers will have done their research about the local area, decided what the property is worth to them and have an idea of what they are prepared to pay but hope they can get away with less. The vendor also hopes to get the full asking price, but understands that they may need to accept a lower offer. The common ground between these two is where negotiation comes in. Negotiation is sometimes about making compromises. It is about dialogue or multilogue. For the

Table 0.1 Contributors to the negotiation process

Role	Particular skill in the negotiation process
Librarian/Head of information department	Maintains an overview of the variety of the resources and can compare contract terms and prices with other products. If heading a team, will know who else can contribute to the negotiation process
Budget holder (if not same as above)	Liaises with other team members to set the budget, looks at past years' prices and estimates future spending, obtains quotes for forthcoming years
Procurement officer	Possesses expertise in procurement, not just information. Has good understanding of contracts
Product user	Understands the strengths and weaknesses of the product and can feed this back to the nominated negotiator. Has a good idea of the value of the product to the work, research or study that they do. Can see if contract permits users to do what is needed by their organization
IT professional	Can assist the information professional with compatibility and reliability issues, and may be able to provide usage statistics if they cannot be provided by the publisher or product itself
In-house trainer	Will have insights into the ease of use (or otherwise) of the product and will have had opportunities for close contact with end-users

information professional it is often not only about negotiating with the publisher, it is also about negotiating with internal people such as budget holders. For the publisher it is about targets, believing in the value of the product and maintaining a good relationship with the purchaser.

Negotiation can be seen as a single event. However, it is far more than that. Compared to a one-off purchase, the nature of an online subscription means that negotiations are likely to be held at intervals, possibly over decades. If a deal is done aggressively in one year, this can impact on the success of negotiations in future years. If there are reasons for wanting to get costs down aggressively in one year, then these need to be explained to the representative and the purchaser has to understand that if the representative is going to meet their demands that year, then they may well need to be the understanding party the next year. From the representative's point of view, if they are asking for a massive price increase or reducing accessibility, then they need extensive powers of explanation and cannot expect this type of change to take place every year.

Sustainable negotiation has the aim of reaching a mutually acceptable agreement. It is not about one side taking advantage of the other. Otherwise when it comes to negotiating in subsequent years, the unsuccessful party is likely to be less prone to movement. Negotiation assumes that you know something about what you are negotiating for, and for this reason the chapters that follow emphasize the importance of preparation. Good negotiation requires good communication, by the purchaser of their expectations and desires about the product and by the publisher about how it works, what the product's value is to the particular organization and transparency about cost and function.

Negotiation for online subscriptions therefore creates a circular pattern:

Preparation > Discussion and explanations > Proposals > Bargain > Conclusion

But this pattern can be moulded and adapted according to needs and the skills of the negotiator. For instance, a negotiated deal does not have to have the same contract term length – on one occasion it may be beneficial to negotiate a multi-year deal, on another occasion it may be necessary to renew that same product for just one year.

This negotiation timeline, based on a typical one-year cycle, can be seen in more detail in Appendix 2.

Why negotiate?

There are numerous reasons why so many organizations fail to negotiate a better price or more favourable terms for their subscriptions. One of these reasons is that the amount of time that is likely to be spent may not justify the possible outcome. This is a valid judgement to make, and often leads to the decision that a negotiation is not necessary. Another major reason that people may avoid negotiation is fear; negotiation removes them from their 'comfort' zone and they have to confront the possibility that they might try and fail, appear weak or overbearing, or damage a client–publisher relationship. Other common reasons, hindrances and excuses for not negotiating a better deal include the following:

- In cultures that are used to fixed prices in shops, it is often so much easier just to agree a price rather than face the 'embarrassment' of negotiating.
- There is a common belief that only large companies, large institutions or consortia have the 'clout' to negotiate.
- Standard discounts or terms (e.g. for charities or academic institutions) are taken up rather than pursuing the process further.
- The product only costs a few pounds so it is not worth spending the time on negotiation.
- Some people fear generating a poor relationship with their much-liked representative.
- People sometimes believe that there is no likelihood of success in getting a better deal, so there is no point in trying.
- Information units nearly always have the historical financial model of having mostly purchased hard copy, where prices were far more transparent and/or fixed.
- Lack of time.
- Failure to prepare for a renewal may mean there is either an obligation to renew at any cost or there is insufficient information to support any case other than the asking price and terms.
- There is the misconception that it is only price that can be negotiated. However, often there are other issues with electronic products that can be negotiated, ranging from how the product can be used to where it can be used.
- The electronic product might not be understood by the purchaser so it is simple for the publisher to tell the purchaser about its merits and

for the purchaser to fail to understand how it will add value to their organization.

The last three reasons listed above are where much of the room for negotiation lies, and the following chapters will help with how to better understand a product, how it benefits your organization and how best to prepare, so that you can get the best price and the best terms.

There are many reasons, incentives and attractions why someone should enter into a negotiation for an online subscription, whether it be on a basic or an advanced level:

- The terms in the contract may not match the needs of the organization.
- Both the publisher and the purchaser need to maintain a good relationship and negotiating ensures that both sides are assertive and content with their dealings.
- The proposed cost may be prohibitive and there may be other budgetary constraints.
- The purchaser is having to make decisions about whether to keep a particular subscription.
- There are alternative and/or comparative products on the market.
- Prices are substantially different from what has been paid in past years.
- Positive or negative feedback from users changes the value of the product to an organization.
- The product might be a 'nice to have' and not an essential product.
- If the organization has customers, clients or shareholders, it is likely to have a duty of care to get the best price.
- For a subscription that costs £100,000, just a 1% saving is not insignificant.
- It is hugely rewarding for the information professional to extend terms or reduce cost and it is a measurable means of their worth to their employer.
- The publisher might at least gain some revenue and another customer, where previously the cost or terms had been a barrier to a subscription.

The aim of this book

The aim of this book is to improve the confidence of those involved in the negotiation by explaining the processes that need to be undertaken. Both parties need to feel assertive to get the best results. By achieving a successful outcome the benefits are extensive:

- professional satisfaction
- a financial measure of success to the employer or business
- the best product at the best price for the end-user
- the best terms, enabling the best use of the product for the widest end-user audience
- the avoidance of any last-minute angst in the negotiation process
- the elimination of misunderstandings between purchaser and publisher.

There are no tips here on how to take unfair advantage, on how to be deceitful or generally 'railroad' the other party. Whilst the aim is to go into detail about the negotiation process, it is also to highlight key points so they can be easily remembered, especially in tongue-tied or impasse situations. For the more experienced negotiator this book aims to show them how much they know already and how they can use their knowledge to involve and develop the skills of other people.

Complementary skills

There are many skills that are complementary to those of negotiation, but not all of them can be explored in much detail in this book. Rather, they are subjects in their own right. For example:

- **Communication skills** – Developing effective communication via in-depth training courses can only benefit the understanding between publisher and purchaser in the negotiation process.
- **The selection of products** – The selection of online subscriptions is a whole new skill, but can impact on your negotiations. Being aware of alternative products in the marketplace can aid your negotiation stance.

- **Dynamic of consortia agreements** – This book will not be focusing on multi-party negotiations for consortia, but the tips and guidance offered here will be relevant for whoever is the person nominated to negotiate the deal.
- **Service level agreements (SLAs)** – Although not unique to information products, SLAs are quite common when a large organization purchases software. They are useful when the product is such a key resource that any downtime or access to helpdesks could seriously affect the value of the product to an organization.
- **The law** – Whilst Chapter 2 focuses on the contract and making the negotiator more comfortable with the jargon that they sometimes contain, it will not be a legal interpretation.
- **Putting deals out to tender** – Some organizations, especially government departments, may have obligations to put expenditure over a certain level out to tender. Writing tender documents is a specific skill, and whilst much of the guidance in this book, especially in the section on preparation, will contribute to what to include in such a tender document, the actual writing of a tender notice for electronic subscriptions is only outlined here.
- **Installation of online subscriptions** – IT issues with regard to online subscriptions are not explored here. Many systems are now designed to be easily accessible (e.g. over the internet), and do not require extra levels of expertise. However, it may be that one of an organization's negotiation points is for IP authentication or screen customization, and these and other examples are mentioned in passing later in the book.
- **Budget management** – Managing an information department's budget is a definite skill, and doing it well where there is a large proportion of the budget spent on online resources depends on the manager, or someone in their team, being a good negotiator.

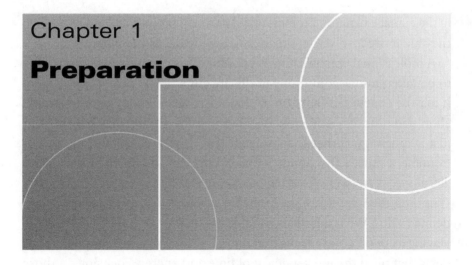

Chapter 1
Preparation

What are the organization's needs?

There is a very strong argument to support the claim that an organization needs a skilled information professional in order to get it the best deals for online databases on the best terms at the best prices. This information professional ideally needs to be close to the management structure in order to do the best job, so as to get the best understanding of the organization's needs. Depending on the size of the organization, this role may be just one strand of a person's job, or it may be undertaken by people dedicated solely to doing negotiation.

Information professionals are increasingly being involved in the decision-making process of the organizations in which they work. Negotiation is just one of the reasons why, ideally, an information professional should have a core understanding of the direction in which the organization is going and how it functions on a day-to-day basis. Some organizations are more open with their employees about what they do and how they do it, whereas in other organizations the information that people need prior to a negotiation taking place may not be freely available to all. Of course the more open environment is the best option, and that is the scenario we have assumed to exist in this chapter. Explaining the importance of negotiation to the management can promote an information professional to a role where they are more involved in organization-wide decision-making.

A professional person's time is valuable. This commodity of time needs to be taken into account fully at the absolute outset of any negotiation. It may be concluded that a small, low-cost subscription is not worth the effort and time of negotiation. A low-value subscription may benefit from just a 'quick try' rather than a detailed course of communications. For example, a single subscription with a list price of £50 might be more aptly 'left alone' as any gains from negotiation would be outweighed by the time spent, or time spent might be better applied to subscriptions over a defined value. What this 'defined value' is remains up to each organization. Having a cut-off point means that human resources can be applied to the deals that need the most amount of time and energy. Focusing on those subscriptions with a higher value (both in cost and in importance to the organization) or complexity of contract is likely to produce the best results.

Understanding the needs of an organization involves the choice of products to fit the purpose of the organization. While product selection is a topic and skill in its own right, knowledge of how the organization functions and uses the products can only help in the negotiation. This applies not only to the information professional and purchaser but to the salesperson and publisher alike. There may be reasons why each party in the negotiation is unable to divulge information about the organization or intended use of the product, but at least some degree of openness in this area avoids any chance of buying/selling the wrong product or getting the product on terms are that not best suited to how it needs to be used.

There are usually degrees to which an organization needs a product. Understanding whether a product is an item which is essential, liked, loathed, a 'nice to have', or 'useful but could live without', can help the negotiator decide on the value of the product and whether that value matches the asking price and terms. Good preparation can help answer these questions and provide a firm foundation for the negotiation stage later on.

A new subscription

A new subscription, as opposed to a renewal, involves a few extra stages in the preparation process.

Locating products

Information about what products exist can be gathered from a wide variety of sources, ranging from personal experience, approaching publishers, flyers, attending shows, consulting users within the organization who have worked previously at similar places to consulting other information professionals. When using this latter process, be receptive to feedback from peers as certain information about the product, both positive and negative, will be useful in the negotiation process.

The trial

The most obvious stage when considering a new product is the trial. Carrying out a proper trial potentially involves a huge investment of time. If there is the luxury of an unlimited budget and unlimited time, then doing a trial to see whether the product would suit the organization's needs without any further stages is fine. However most organizations do not have the luxury of unlimited budgets and time.

While some 'quick and dirty' trials can speedily exclude a product from consideration, poorly planned trials can lead to end-users getting 'addicted' to the new product without there necessarily being sufficient funds to pay for it. Having end-user addicts can put the purchaser in a weaker position when negotiating, as failing to come to agreement can make enemies among the addicts. Another downside of going into a trial without any planning is that it is beneficial to trial products that perform similar roles at the same time. This avoids end-user apathy with trial following trial, or even the wrong end-user being involved in the wrong trial. Multi-product trials also have the benefit of providing benchmarks for each database. Therefore, to ensure being in a better position for negotiation it is best to follow the steps below:

• Get some outline information on what the product does and what it contains.

- Are there any products that perform a similar function that should be trialled at the same time?
- Decide how and by whom the product will be used.
- Obtain a rough price and compare with budget or price of comparative product.
- If the price is not hugely out of reach, then arrange a suitable date and length for the trial. Too long a trial and users tend to forget to give feedback; too short and a busy spell might mean they are unable to use the product in the given timeframe.
- Decide who should be involved in the trial. Are these 'regulars' who can be relied upon to give good feedback, or are instructions needed on what sort of feedback is expected from them and by when?
- If the product is complex, arrange a demonstration or training session from the publisher for those who are going to be involved in the trial. Less complex databases may benefit from an overview by the information professional so they are not oversold. Some people involved in trials may never actually invest time past the demonstration stage and so make decisions based on this session alone.
- If trialling more than one product for the same function or similar content, compile a very brief table of the advantages and disadvantages of each product, using common parameters ranging from content and breadth to searchability.
- Decide if those involved in the trial should know how much the product costs so they can make a fairer assessment of its value.
- Set a calendar reminder a week before the end of the trial and contact those who have been involved, asking for feedback.
- Having got some feedback, look at the contract and check that the permissions in it allow the product to be used as desired.
- Note any feedback that might be useful in any negotiation (e.g. about desired changes to the interface, performance, etc.).
- Record the fact that a trial was undertaken, the outcome and the reasons behind that decision and whether it is something that should be revisited in a few years' time.
- From this point on, armed with sufficient information, the regular negotiation process can be followed.

Comparing products

In some situations a product is the only one that contains the desired information. Where there are alternatives, just knowing that these exist can put an organization into a stronger negotiating position. This subject is explored in more detail later in this chapter.

Commencing a subscription

If it is decided to subscribe, this should be done on a timetable that suits the subscribing organization. There is little point in starting a subscription if it cannot be used due to lack of training, staff or IT issues. It is not uncommon for subscriptions to commence, only to fail to be used for several months. This under-use can affect everything from usage levels upon which prices might be based, to perception in and outside the organization on how online subscriptions are managed.

If the decision is that the product is highly desirable, but there are concerns about over-expenditure in any particular financial year, there are solutions that can suit both purchaser and publisher. Where the preferred subscription model is not an option for the subscriber in the short term, making this clear to the publisher will ensure a greater chance of good short- and long-term deals. Alternative solutions to the desired subscription model, which can be suggested by either party, include:

- initially subscribing for a period shorter than a year
- initially subscribing on a different pricing model (e.g. pay-as-you go) with the intention of reviewing this
- postponing the start date of the subscription so that it goes into a new financial year (sometimes the publisher is willing to extend the trial for even several months so that there is a continuous service)
- paying instalments
- initially subscribing for a select group with the intention of widening access at a later date.

Renewing a subscription

When renewing a subscription to an electronic database the route of least resistance is to renew like for like with no quibbles over the price or terms.

When to conduct a review of a renewal

On a practical level it is often not possible to do much more than a simple renewal every year. However, reasons for reviewing a products' worth to the organization are often prompted by any one or more of the following:

- downward pressure on the budget
- a price increase larger than expected
- the removal of some key content from the database
- the addition of some key content to a database subscribed to, which now means it overlaps or even replaces the subscription under scrutiny
- the existence of a competitor product
- poor usage statistics
- a change in the direction or focus of the organization which results in different information requirements
- a major interface upgrade to the product which requires a substantial end-user education programme
- the departure or arrival of key individuals or end-users in the organization
- the migration of the content from one platform (e.g. CD-ROM) to another (e.g. internet), often resulting in a change to the access model, currency and IT support required.

When time does permit, or when the decision for a review has been made, then information:

- about the product
- who uses it
- how much it is used
- how easy it is to use
- what it costs
- how it is valued

is essential in forming a strong position for negotiating a renewal of the contract. Renewing a subscription takes into account the history of the subscription and is often based upon the previous contract terms and price. Therefore getting the right deal will set the standard for future negotiations.

Termination clauses

There are sections in the contract about renewals (or the rather the decision not to renew) and these will be explored in the next chapter, which aims to unravel the complexities of the contract. On the preparation side, it is essential that the section on renewal or termination is examined closely so that the organization is not placed under an obligation to renew. Even if the intention is to renew, as soon as there is an obligation to do so then the purchaser is automatically in a weaker position.

Gathering feedback about the product

Depending on the value of the contract, the publisher or sales representative will keep in touch with the organization to varying degrees throughout the subscription period. To ensure there are no 'nasty surprises' nearer renewal time, lines of communication should be kept well and truly open. Representatives should not wait for the customer to complain about issues such as poor performance or changes to content. The onus should be on them, thereby building up a level of trust that will encourage the negotiation process to go all the more smoothly. Likewise, the purchaser should be open about their experiences, including praising the product or providing constructive feedback. Leaving all the communication to the last minute results in one side being wrong-footed and often puts them on the defensive, meaning that the focus is not on the renewal but on other issues that could have been resolved or highlighted earlier.

It is best to start the information-gathering process about how the product is valued inside the organization as these experiences will be most relevant. This stage should take place well before any renewal date, to take into account the fact that some people who need to be involved or consulted may have holidays or other commitments and that the information is needed well before any meeting or discussion about renewal with the publisher. Ways of gathering this information internally can take anything from ten minutes to days of detailed work. How in-depth the information gathered needs to be depends on the value of the product, the amount of time available and the number of users. When conducting end-user research care must be taken not to phrase questions so as to worry the interviewee. Some users may have a great attachment to a product and may become concerned that it could be taken away from them.

Gathering feedback can include:

- automatic access to online usage statistics and/or search strategies
- mini surveys using e-mail. For example, some e-mail systems have a voting button option which means the user just has to make only one click; a simple survey might include the options:
  - essential
  - useful but not essential
  - nice to have
  - not needed/used
- more detailed surveys, either electronic or on paper
- comments made to information staff
- brief interviews, either in person or on the telephone, perhaps as short as 'Do you have any strong feelings or experiences about product X?'
- attending or organizing a meeting for end-users to do a refresher presentation about the product and eliciting feedback at the same time
- reference to e-mail communications with representatives and users over the previous term, relating to the performance of the product, upgrades and so forth.

For the more substantial subscriptions it is worth keeping an easily accessible file, either in hard copy or electronically. It may be that copies of the contract are kept in the same file, with a separate section or folder for feedback, including the noting of any downtime or other technical problems, plus any major testimonials. Some online catalogues have a section for who requested the product and who authorized its purchase. Any discussion should include the person who requested the product, if they are still with the organization. The online catalogue record may also have other fields which you choose to use to help with the renewal process, including entering a date for when you want to start the renewal examination process as opposed to the actual renewal date, the ability to view percentage increases over a number of years and many other options.

Some attention can be paid to other experiences by those outside the organization, via either networking, user groups, e-mail discussion lists or references. User groups are a very good way of airing praise and grievance alike. Sometimes they are convened by the publisher, sometimes by a group of users. These are good way for purchasers to know if the publisher listens to their customers and acts upon suggestions. For the publisher it is a way to diffuse any possible discontent as well as advertise any developments planned for the product. E-mail discussion lists should be used with caution, as they can turn into unproductive streams of moans. In addition, it is not always obvious who receives the e-mail or has access to the discussion archive. It could include the publisher.

Is the price fair?

Judging whether a price quoted is fair is one of the most difficult aspects of a renewal. Some publishers have list prices that are widely advertised, so there will be at least common starting points for all customers. All too often prices fail to be transparent or publicly available. Where some transparency exists, prices may be based on a variety of criteria, including:

- the number of named users – including power users versus occasional users
- the number of terminals
- the number of passwords or concurrent users
- the number of modules
- the amount downloaded
- the number of locations/offices/sites.

However, the organization may find that the model used by the publisher does not suit them. Some publishers are more flexible than others in recognizing this. A common complaint among purchasers is that they feel the publisher asks them to pay what they think they can afford, rather than any other transparent model. It is up to the purchaser to communicate their concerns to the publisher or salesperson and ask upon what model the pricing is based. On the other side, the publisher needs to be aware that the purchaser has to be convinced that the price is fair, for example for negotiating and justifying the expenditure within their own organization. Some purchasers can feel reassured about the publisher's pricing models, either through personal experience, communication with their representative, discussion with colleagues, or because the publisher has signed up to an industry code of practice that might include the issues of fair and transparent pricing.

Some contracts contain a clause which forbids discussion about what price was agreed outside the contracting organization. Even if there is no clause forbidding discussion about price, if an organization gets what it considers to be a good deal, revealing this to another organization may make future successful deals less likely. In the commercial sector in particular, there may be competitors with whom open discussion is difficult. It may be felt that revealing what price was achieved might hinder a competitive advantage that was gained by getting such a good deal. There is also the difficulty of obtaining a price comparison for the more unique organizations. If discussion among peers of the exact price paid is not possible, then an alternative can be to discuss the price change. This can be a way to gauge whether the same principle is being applied to other organizations. For example, an information professional at one organization may mention to their equivalent at another organization that they are being asked for a 20% hike in their subscription cost to product X for no additional level of service or content.

From the purchaser's point of view it is better to keep renewal discussions separate from demonstrations about product enhancements. Attending a meeting about renewal, only to be faced with heaps of praise about recent improvements or what is planned for the product in the future can take the focus away from the subject of renewal and turn the meeting into one where the purchaser feels they cannot argue about large price increases.

The takeover of a product by another publisher

The takeover of a product by another publisher strikes fear into the information professional's heart. Consequences can include the product ceasing, being integrated into another product, having a massive price hike or, more rarely, the change being hardly noticeable. When a takeover situation arises, the information professional has to deal with two publishers for a certain period of time to ensure a smooth handover.

The information professional can take the initiative here and make some assumptions. They can communicate with the new publisher and say something like 'I assume this takeover will not affect us too much on a day-to-day basis and that prices will not materially change?' The response to this assumptive question will need to be recorded for any subsequent negotiations. Most jurisdictions also operate a data protection system where details of a subscription, including the price that was paid, cannot be handed over to the purchaser without the consent of the subscriber. The information professional needs to decide whether it is in their best interests for this information to be handed over or not. One course of action can be for the subscriber to await the proposed price from the new publisher, and if is dramatically higher than what was paid to the previous publisher, then they can reveal the basis of their previous subscription.

Where the product is integrated into another product, the response of the negotiator depends on whether they already subscribe to the new product. Where they already have a subscription to the new product, an examination of the pricing models of each version will reveal what sorts of negotiation will need to take place. If the pricing models of the old product and the new product are the same, such as pay-as-you-go, then negotiation will be minimal. If the pricing model for the old product was a fixed 'all you can eat' model, and the new product is pay-as-you-go, then this may pose a problem for the organization. In some instances the purchaser is the gainer, for example where they had paid an annual subscription for the product and it is incorporated into another product they subscribe to it but at no extra cost. The contract also needs to be examined to ensure that the information can continue to be used in the same way as it has been previously.

Renewal summary

In summary, a renewal can be as simple or as involved as an organization wants it to be, but as a general rule, the more preparation that is put in, the greater the rewards. Sometimes the decision to review a product's renewal can be that of the information professional, sometimes it is driven by outside forces, such as the product changing hands or content within the product being removed.

Understanding a product and how the organization intends to use it

Many negotiators in an organization are user–negotiators, that is, they both use the product and negotiate the deal for it. However, in larger organizations the task of procurement may be a specialized one and the negotiator has no personal experience of the product. There are merits in both systems. If a user–negotiator is involved, then the amount of preparation to understand the product is minimal and can, if time is limited, be almost negligible as their experience can be drawn upon in the later stages of the negotiations without any further work. If the person is a procurement specialist, they will be expert at getting the best deals but will not be able to draw upon valuable information about the product and how it is used without prior research. The advantage of having this information about the product is that the purchaser can be more assertive in the meeting, can deal better with statements or claims by the publisher and knows whether offers about free extra content, service or access are what the organization needs. If there is to be a meeting and an end-user is to be included, then they should be forewarned and advised on what they are expected to contribute to the discussion. Where the end-user and purchaser are different people, then the negotiator needs to have certain information to hand. This can be presented in tabular form, as shown in Table 1.1.

The publisher or sales representative also has a key role in gathering information, ensuring that they keep up to date about who they are liaising with, whether their client has experienced any changes to their structure or needs. Understanding the strengths and weaknesses of competitor products is also a bonus and can pre-empt the observations made about them by the purchaser at any renewal discussions.

Table 1.1   Example of the information needed by non-user negotiators

Product X is a news database covering the last 90 days, accessible via the internet to named individuals who have passwords. There are 5000 aggregated news sources. This product was chosen as the result of a trial of four news databases three years previously. The terms of the licence do not permit dissemination of the information to other individuals.

Product X	Result	Example
Reliability/ performance/ usability/ growth	Excellent performance, usability could be improved	Feedback from some users indicates that they are confused by how to search for archived materials and would like to be able to disseminate information more widely. No new modules added
Who uses the product	Ten core users, five other users	The marketing department have expressed interest in having access for at least one user, maybe up to three if the price is not more than £1500 in total
Cost versus charge back	We do not charge back for this	In the previous year the cost was £1000 per user, but as we had ten or more users the cost was reduced to £900 per user
Renewal dates and contract length	Due to renew on 1 June	There are competitor products on the market so do not renew for more than one year unless an exceptional deal is offered
Usage statistics	Supplied by the publisher	Usage levels are exceptionally low amongst non-core users
Relationships with other parts of the organization	Marketing and Department Y	Marketing pay to advertise on the publishers' website. Mr Z in Department Y contributes articles

Continued on next page

Table 1.1 *Continued*

Product X	Result	Example
Alternative products	There are three competitor products, at least one of which we'd be happy to subscribe to	Product M at £850 per user but only a 60-day archive; Product Q at £25,000 per organization for unlimited number of users; Product V at £500 registration fee plus £4 per news story
Overlapping modules	None	We do not subscribe to the optional archive which includes our 90 days' subscription plus news since 1980
Value to the organization	Medium	News is an essential resource but as there are alternatives and relatively few users, it is not a high-value product

Reliability/performance/usability/growth

There is no reason to pay a premium price if the product is not performing at its optimum. If an organization is unable to use a product due to downtime which is the fault of the publisher, then the publisher should acknowledge this in a variety of ways. This might include agreeing to extend the term of the subscription or reducing the renewal price by an agreed percentage.

If there are reasons why the product fails that are the fault of the subscriber, then there may be other options that the publisher can offer. Some products can be hosted by either the publisher or the subscriber. If one method is not working for the subscriber, then exploring the alternative can be part of the negotiation. Format options are another way in which reliability can be improved, for example moving over from CD-ROM to internet or vice versa.

Reliability has different shades to it. It can be viewed as accuracy, speed of access or general 'uptime'. For some organizations reliability has a business imperative: for example, a stockbroking firm needs real-time stock prices in order to carry on business. In instances such as these there will be various onuses on the reliability of the publisher, the telecommunications company and the in-house IT team. It may be that penalty clauses exist in the main contract. If not, it may be necessary to draw up a separate service level agreement. Where an organization does express the importance of reliability, it is also demonstrating to the publisher how important the product is to them – in effect, that they would find it difficult to manage without it.

Another aspect to consider is whether the product has matured over the previous contract term. Most products will develop over time and a certain amount of new information, added features and content should be expected. Completely new modules or a new area of content, however, will need to be treated differently. The subscriber may not value the new content or developments and, if this is the case, can argue that they should not be penalized by large increases in prices.

Who uses the product?

Who has access to the electronic resource that is being renewed or newly purchased is open to question. Each publisher has its own definition of who a user is. Information professionals are often battling with users to explain all these differences and to ensure they do not hand over user names and passwords when they should not be doing so. The information professional is usually the one in the position to decide who has access, based on a combination of need and cost. Changing the number or extent of users is a key part of the negotiation territory. There is much debate about to whom the publisher directs their energy when trying to sell the product. There is an increasing trend by publishers to contact end-users directly, often to the frustration of information professionals who are trying to co-ordinate a wide variety of subscriptions. Whatever the definition of user, there are common questions that need to be clarified:

- Does the information need to be disseminated outside the organization and, if so, is this permitted under the terms of the contract?
- Does the information need to be disseminated by permitted users to non-permitted users within the organization (e.g. searchers passing

on information to those who just refer to the data)?

- How will non-users experience information that is passed on to them (e.g. clicking on links which will prompt them for login IDs)?
- What training is offered to enable users to get the most out of the product?
- What alternative pricing models are there? Is the one that the organization is part of still the right one?
- Does the publisher amend its pricing according to the type or skill of the user or user group?
- If so, does the publisher have different pricing for those who use the product heavily, compared to the occasional user?

Everyone

At one extreme is the interpretation that, in theory, if the resource is accessed via the internet via silent authentication, then any single member of staff can access it, deliberately or not, from cleaners and secretaries to research staff and visitors. This is most commonly called a site licence. Most publishers are realistic and will not base their charge on everyone. The usual situation is that they will charge for 'core' or 'power' users or those in a specific department most 'likely' to use the product. The advantage of this model is that the administration for the information department is minimal: there is no need to notify the publisher of individual leavers and joiners. One disadvantage is that it can be difficult to determine who is using the product unless there is good software that distinguishes one user from another. Another disadvantage is keeping on top of any product-awareness training, if, in theory, anyone in the organization can access a product. While this may be an advantage, having a clear idea of the real users to ensure they know where to access the product is vital to ensure the most value is obtained from the product. The 'everyone' access can also extend to every site and every office within an organization and to home or business travel access, or can be restricted to one location and no out-of-office access. Therefore, if on the surface it seems the organization has an 'everyone' subscription, questions to explore in the negotiation process include:

- What is the price based upon?
- What if one of the users wants to access this information outside the organization (e.g. from home or on a business trip)?
- Is this a single-site or a multi-site licence?

One named user

At the other end of the spectrum of access is the one named user. Sometimes the user may be the information professional themselves, or may be a specialist within the organization. If the product is used by a named user whose role it is to disseminate the information from the product to others within the organization, then this needs to match the permissions in the contract. The organization also needs to have in place a system that alerts them if someone leaves the organization. It may then be that either the access needs to be reassigned to another individual or that a decision is made about whether it is necessary to renew. Tools such as catalogue circulation lists can often be used for electronic resources, not just hard copy. The publisher can help with subscriptions as they may notice when a product is no longer being used and contact the purchaser just to check that everything is fine.

Journals have some issues all of their own. With some journals there may be a 'free' online subscription to a named user. How flexible the publisher is about named user access varies. There are known instances where the hard-copy journal is addressed to 'The Librarian' and so the online access has to match this, even if it is just a token job title and the person or role does not really exist. It is up to each organization to decide whether to take advantage of free access. It is not obligatory and can take up much of an information professional's time sorting out the various subscriptions and assigning them to individuals. An efficient, but not timely, way of dealing with this is that when an organization is made aware that online access is an option this is noted on the catalogue record and activated only when someone expresses an interest in it. It is then assigned to that individual. If time or urgent access at short notice is an issue, then assignment of the access does need to be planned ahead of any enquiries from potential users. Subscribers should make the publisher aware of nonuse of an electronic subscription if the publisher argues that development of online access has resulted in a large price increase for the hard copy.

Questions to ask about named users include:

- How easy is it to assign access to another person if the named user leaves?
- Can there be temporary reassignment of access if the named user goes on maternity leave?
- What about access when the named user is on holiday?
- To what extent can the named user disseminate information within and outside the organization?
- For e-journals, if an agent is involved, what level of support can be expected for contract negotiation, troubleshooting and set-up?

Concurrent users

Concurrent usage is a fairly popular model with subscribers. As with a site licence, the theory is that anyone within an organization can access the product, but there is a limit put on the number of people who do so at any one time. A good salesperson will point out the number of times users, or a percentage of attempted users, have tried to access the product only to be told that they cannot because the maximum number of users are already using it. This negative experience is often called 'lockout'. In a negotiation process it is important for the organization to have any feedback from those people to whom complaints or queries about access would be directed, whether this is an IT helpdesk or the information professional. It may also be necessary to contact key users to ascertain from them their experiences about access. Once an organization requests information about lockouts it has to be prepared to deal with the response. A quick look at the budget to see whether expenditure on an additional concurrent user is an option should be explored in conjunction with how important it is for individuals to access the product at the first attempt.

Questions to ask about concurrent usage include:

- How important is it for users to have access at the first attempt?
- Is the concurrent usage specific to one site or is it multi-site?

- Does the number of concurrent users need to go up or down?
- What experiences of lockouts are users getting?
- Is there a point where it is more economical to switch to an alternative pricing plan if one is available?

Group of users

A defined group may be given access. This might include all the information professionals within an organization, or a specific department or level. The reasons for only giving a group access may be due to the subject nature of the product, for cost reasons or to ensure that those accessing it are experts rather than occasional users. In the negotiation process the publisher will often try to broaden this group of users to gain more revenue. The purchaser will either want to broaden the group at little extra cost or to keep the group at its minimum.

Tied or bundled usage

In some instances the business model used by the publisher ties the electronic version into the hard-copy version. This often applies to journals. There are instances where it is not possible to subscribe to the electronic version without having at least one subscription to the hard-copy version. Publishers usually argue that the hard copy is their main revenue stream and they need to protect this as it is also often tied in with advertising. The unsuitability of a bundled package may be an area for negotiation, either undoing the bundle or explaining that one of the two formats is not something that is desirable for the organization. Sometimes it is possible to get the same resource from a third-party aggregator without the same bundling issue.

Another issue with bundling is that there are often different taxes applied to electronic as opposed to hard-copy resources. For example, in the UK a book does not attract value added tax (VAT), but where a book or looseleaf is supplied with a 'free' CD-ROM, the publisher has to assign a value to it for tax purposes as the electronic component does incur VAT. Some bundled deals may be very attractive and offer the subscriber fewer invoices, a known cost regardless of how much of the electronic resource is used or how much of the hard copy is ordered, and ultimately fewer meetings and negotiations.

Cost versus charge back

Some subscriptions have an upfront cost, some have a cost based on usage, some have a combination of the two. Each organization will have its own model about whether the cost for a product is absorbed or is charged out to a third party in some way. Most online products have a reporting module where costs increase according to the level of usage. Some of these tools can even be integrated into an organization's own billing system. However, organizations owe a duty of care to their clients, students, public or shareholders to keep costs down. If the information unit is not having to pay for a product because costs are passed on to a third party, then the negotiation does not have to be quite so tough. Some organizations are known to actually make a profit out of some online products, but this is up to each organization. Note should be taken of any legislation, charters or codes of practice to which the organization is subject that may affect the extent to which they can pass on costs. Where an organization does not charge back for a product, it can remind the publisher or salesperson that this is the case. Where an organization does charge back, it can point out that this is not for the purpose of taking advantage.

One of the most difficult scenarios is where the cost of the product increases depending on bands of usage, rather than a cost per identifiable item. For example, a product might cost £1000 for 5000 hits a year, £3000 for 20,000 hits a year, and £5000 for 50,000 hits a year. Negotiating on this basis is virtually impossible and an alternative model should be sought unless the purchaser is very clear about their likely levels of usage. If there is no alternative, there are arguments that can be used in the negotiation process. From the purchaser's point of view, they are penalized for the popularity a product might gain, and feel that they cannot promote the use of that product even though they are paying for something they are not getting the most out of for fear of going into the next band. There is also the assumption by the publisher that the number of hits is an indication of the popularity of a product, whereas any information professional knows that a higher number of hits can actually mean that the user is struggling with finding what they are after and so are having to view more pages and do more searches.

How and when the cost is paid is also an area for negotiation. Different payment methods and times suit the publisher and the purchaser in different ways. For example, it may be reassuring for the publisher to be paid by direct debit, but it may not be an option favoured by the organization's accounts department. Listed below are payment options that can all be explored, each having its own value to each party and some of which can be combined with others (e.g. monthly payments by direct debit):

- direct debit or standing order
- cheque or bankers' draft
- annually up-front
- monthly or quarterly
- pre-pay accounts where there are unit costs
- usage invoices or pay-as-you-go.

This is just one example of where, in the negotiation process, a solution can be found that means neither party is losing out, but both gain.

Renewal dates and contract length

Most electronic subscriptions run for a period of one year, although there are alternatives. Most publishers would be willing to have a subscription run for less than one year and have at least some revenue rather than none, if that were the choice for the purchaser. Reasons for having a subscription run for less than a year include:

- tying the subscription in with others from the same publisher
- insufficient funds in this financial year
- arranging the subscription to end at a particular date to either consolidate subscriptions or spread them over different time periods
- treating the subscription as a lengthy trial period
- the product ceasing
- changing over to an alternative product.

Similarly, there are reasons for extending the subscription period. Often the payment terms remain the same, and sums are still due annually or monthly, but in some instances payment for years ahead might be due. Reasons for extending the subscription period include:

- tying the subscription in with others from the same publisher
- publishers being prepared to do good deals where they are assured a revenue stream for the next few years
- publishers and purchasers saving time for future negotiations
- planning ahead can help with the setting of budgets.

If an organization agrees to tie itself in for a number of years, it is usually acknowledging to the publisher the importance of the product.

Usage statistics

Usage statistics can be a valuable tool in the negotiation process, but they are a potential double-edged sword. Low usage can be an indication of how little the product is valued within the organization and how the cost should reflect this. High levels of usage can indicate one of two things: either that the product is highly valued or that users are taking their time to find what they want within the product. From the purchaser's standpoint it is desirable to be able to view statistics independently of having to ask the publisher. This is often possible with the larger databases and publishers. Once the statistics have been viewed, the purchaser can then decide on whether to raise the issue of usage levels at the negotiation stage, bearing in mind too that the publisher may independently raise the issue of usage.

Some usage statistics are detailed enough to tell an organization who uses the product most frequently and will aid the negotiator in gaining feedback from these individuals. They may show a pattern of core users and occasional users, which is particularly useful if negotiating a licence for named users only. Where a purchaser has to ask the publisher to supply usage statistics, be prepared that these may show an unexpected picture and the publisher will also be privy to that information.

Relationships with other parts of the organization

Knowing whether someone else in the organization has a relationship with the publisher or the particular product can prevent potential embarrassment. It can make for awkward moments during the negotiation process if one party is ignorant of a relationship, and can contribute to internal differences within an organization. The sorts of relationships that might exist include:

- individuals within the organization contributing content to the product
- sponsorship of the organization by the publisher
- advertising by the organization on the product's website
- sponsorship by the organization of a regular feature on the product.

Alternative products

For the salesperson, knowing competitor products and where their own product has comparable strengths and weaknesses prevents any chance of them appearing complacent. If a salesperson appears complacent, then the purchaser may feel uncomfortable about the product's future, especially the publisher's receptiveness to enhancements. A checklist of comparisons includes:

- cost and pricing model options
- currency and frequency of updates
- depth/archive of content
- breadth of content
- functionality
- search options, interface and usability
- access, including logins, silent authentication, remote access.

Some of these issues will be more important than others to each individual organization. Putting the criteria for comparison in order of importance will help show the key differences sooner and save time in further examination if it soon becomes clear that one product is less suitable on a key issue.

Overlapping modules

Where a product is sold in modules the common elements of the different modules subscribed to by the organization need to be examined. For example, the same information might be repeated across a variety of modules and the organization is, in effect, paying for it several times over. Any discount that the publisher operates for subscribing to a range of modules should not only reflect the volume of modules but the fact that information is re-used.

The same principle may apply to different products by the same publisher, but where some of same content is reproduced in each of the products. The issue that should be applied here is whether it is fair for a subscriber to be charged twice for the same information, even though it is on a different platform. One way of resolving this situation is via a reduction in price for one or all of the affected products.

Value to the organization

The value of a particular online product to an organization will vary from institution to institution. A database on company information will have more value in a firm that does corporate research as its main business than to a school library where it is of more novelty or educational value. The value argument is therefore a relative one, but can be difficult to convey. An organization may have revealed how much it values a product in the course of their relationship, through negotiating a service level agreement or explaining how it intends to use the product. If there is a competitor product on the market and changing systems would not be a strategic headache, then the value of the product is going to be less. If the product is unique or there are lots of users who express their liking of that particular interface or product, then the value is likely to be higher.

Plotting of all of an organization's online subscriptions on a grid (see Figure 1.1) will give you an idea of how robust a negotiation might need to be. The grey area contains those products that have high value and fewer options. The letters in circles denote the plotting of specific products. Plotting on the grid can either be done visually or with the aid of the questions below.

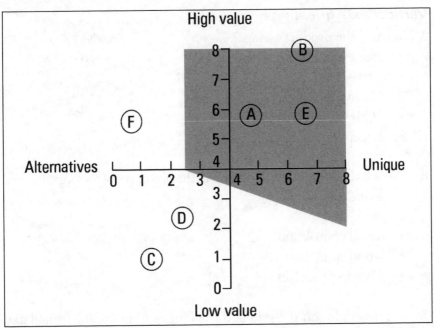

Figure 1.1   Plotting the value of a range of products to an organization

Horizontal axis questions

1   To what degree are there alternative products?
   - None = 4
   - One = 3
   - Two = 2
   - Three = 1
   - Four or more alternatives = 0

2   How easy would migration from one product be for the organization, taking into account the number of users to train and technical issues?
   - Not applicable as no alternative is available = 4
   - Difficult = 3
   - Small amount of complexity = 2
   - Easy = 1
   - Virtually no impact = 0

Vertical axis questions

A   What is the product's usage?
  * None = 0
  * Low = 1
  * Medium = 2
  * High = 3
  * Exceptionally high/constant = 4

B   What is the content's relationship to the objectives of the organization?
  * None = 0
  * Fringe = 1
  * Small contribution = 2
  * Good contribution = 3
  * Core to objectives = 4

To be able to plot on the grid add the figures from the horizontal axis questions to get a range from 0 to 8 and do the same for the vertical axis questions. Drawing up and across the grid will show you where the product falls.

Tender requirements

Some organizations are under an obligation to tender for any contracts over a certain amount. This particularly applies to government institutions and public bodies, but can be the conscious policy of any organization. Issues to take into account if subject to the requirement to tender are:

* Where are you starting from? Do you already subscribe to something or is it a new service?
* What does the product need to achieve for the organization?
* What is the amount over which the organization has to tender, or do all services have to be tendered for? If the price is just over a tender threshold, use this as a bargaining tool.

- To whom is the tender document being issued? Is there only one contender?
- Is there an advantage in advising each publisher who else is involved in the tender process?
- How does the tendering process have to fit in with the organization's budget year? This could mean that prices need to be agreed over a year ahead of the start of subscription.
- Upon what criteria does the organization award a tender? Is it solely on price or are service levels also included?
- Who else in the organization (ranging from lawyers to procurement specialists) is involved in the tender process?
- Is there an option to have a 'preferred bidder' where the most appropriate resource has been identified?

What also needs to be considered is whether there is a legal or regulatory requirement to publish a tender, especially one over a certain value. For example, in the European Union (EU) all public tenders exceeding specific contract values must be published in the *Supplement to the Official Journal* (OJ S). The contract value thresholds above which an invitation to tender must be published are set out in EU Directives.[1]

A typical structure of a tender document might be as follows:

Contact details – including who to contact in the event of further questions
Date of issue of tender
Date for submission
Date by which responses to a tender might be expected
Method by which submissions should be made (e.g. e-mail, web-form, presentation or letter)
Whether the tender is public knowledge or in confidence
Expenses – some wording to make it clear if those tendering can expect expenses to be reimbursed
Pricing structure and duration – how the information about pricing should be presented, especially if asking for more than one model of access, and how long it is expected the publisher will hold that price and/or terms

Treatment of tender decision – this part allows the organization putting out the tender to explain (or not) how they intend to judge any tenders, with an indication of how much weight might be placed on price as opposed to wider contract terms. Mention whether, after an initial phase, meetings or another process might take place. Alternatively, a clause keeping options open can be here, for example 'we reserve the right to accept any part, or all of any tender at our discretion'. In addition, the likelihood of supplying any feedback to unsuccessful tenderers will manage expectations about future communications.

References – if the issuer wants to get feedback from current customers, then the tenderer may be asked to supply contact details of two or three customers with a similar background to their own

Disclaimer – saying that the tendering organization accepts no liability regarding the information in the tender document

Requirements

- what is in place at the moment, if anything?
- the extent of the subscription in terms of users and locations
- what is wanted in terms of content, searching, integration and functionality?
- the audience for whom it is wanted
- what the product or content needs to achieve for the organization?
- any software or hardware issues
- key dates, such as a current contract expiry date.

Agents

Some organizations employ agents to manage their subscriptions. Agents are most often employed for journals and this type of management might extend to their online equivalents. Some agents charge a fee, which is usually a percentage of the cost of the journal; others do not charge their clients but generate their income via discounts from the publishers. With this sort of relationship there may not be an incentive to obtain good deals that benefit the purchaser. It is up to each organization to decide whether high-value electronic subscriptions should remain with an agent or whether the negotiation should be bought in-house. One option is to build in incentive into the contract with the agent, for example a percentage of the amount they manage to get off the list price. However, this does not take into account other aspects of the subscription, such as access and amending contract terms. Communicating requirements to the agent might take just as much time as liaising directly with the publisher as it is rare that each subscription has the same requirements across an organization.

From the publisher's standpoint, they often like to retain some direct contact with their subscribers as they benefit by gaining a better understanding of the organization's requirements and can ensure the product is meeting their subscriber's needs. It can be tempting, if an agent is employed, to cut the cords of direct communication between publisher and subscriber, but this need not be the case if the subscriber considers they would benefit from such a relationship. Agents are also made aware by consortium organizers of any subscription agreements that might be available for their clients. For an organization that does not have either a large enough team or the right mix of skills, an agent will have much experience to offer, ranging from contract interpretation to setting up access to online resources. The role of an agent is therefore a complex network of relationships and relies on good communication between all parties.

Quotes from the publisher

It is desirable for the negotiator to obtain a quote from the publisher prior to any meeting or the final stages of the process. This figure needs to be compared with the price paid in the previous subscription term and with the product as it has or has not matured. The actual negotiation can then be far more productive as there are no 'nasty surprises' to contend with. There is an assumption that price always has to increase year after year, but this is not the case. Exactly what arguments can be used are explored in more detail in Chapter 3 on 'Negotiation'.

A purchaser may ask for more than one quote. The reasons for this include:

- to compare a multi-year deal with a single year's renewal price, in anticipation of zero or minimal price increases over the multi-year period
- to quote for different pricing models or levels of access (e.g. an existing subscription might be for a limited number of people, and if the price is right a site licence may be something the organization is interested in)
- to quote for different or additional modules
- to quote for taking additional resources from the same publisher.

If a publisher or salesperson refuses to be pinned down prior to any detailed negotiations then it may be possible to elicit other comments, such as 'the price is likely to be similar to that which was paid last year'. It is also useful for the publisher to know what the purchaser is expecting. This will then ensure that neither party is dealt a complete surprise when the negotiation begins in earnest.

If a quote is given in a currency different from that in which the organization prefers to operate, the purchaser should check with the publisher if alternative currencies are available. Most international publishers are able and happy to issue invoices or statements in different currencies. If the publisher is unable to be flexible on this, the purchaser needs to ensure that their accounts department (or themselves if a sole trader) can deal with this and whether there are any charges involved in paying in a foreign currency. If there are penalties involved in paying the publisher in a foreign currency, then this fact should be noted as a negotiation point.

The quote may originate from a country other than that of the subscriber's own. If a subscribing organization is liable to pay tax on a service, from where the invoice originates may also affect the overall cost. Again some publishers may be in a position to invoice from different countries and thereby offer their subscribers the best deal. This is yet another example of where both parties can gain something for little effort or cost.

Budgetary issues

Managing an information department's budget is a specific skill all of its own. Where there is a large proportion of the budget spent on online resources negotiation of the prices and payment patterns of those resources is very important. There is a certain amount of information that needs to be gathered prior to the negotiation process with regard to the budget:

- Is there a price budgeted for the resource under negotiation?
- What procedures are there if the product goes over budget?
- Have savings elsewhere made this negotiation less imperative?
- Have overspends elsewhere made this negotiation all the more important?
- Are there expectations for the budget to be changed from that which has been planned (e.g. cuts or additions)?

Where budgetary cuts are demanded at short notice accounts departments are often unaware that it is not possible to just cease subscribing to something mid-term, or that the most expensive online item in the budget is also the one that allows the organization to do what it does. This is where internal communication and negotiation come to the fore. There is a certain amount of planning ahead that can be done by the information professional. Cuts may need to be made either because of unplanned overspend on a key item or because of cuts made to the overall budget. One easy and quick way to differentiate the importance of a product is to mark all the online resources with one of three labels: essential, highly valued, nice to have.

Being aware of the budget process within the organization is also another way to assist the information professional in planning ahead. In some organizations draft budgets are submitted months ahead of the new financial year – sometimes as much as six months ahead. This can therefore mean having a good idea of the price for a product that is due for renewal nearer the end of the organization's financial year as much as 18 months ahead of time. How accurate the budget needs to be also depends on how early the negotiation process might start. For instance, estimates based on what was paid in the previous year might be deemed sufficient.

MFP (Most Favoured Position), WAP (Walk Away Position) and BATNA (Best Alternative to a Negotiated Agreement)

With all the information gathered it is then possible for both parties to work out their negotiation parameters. There needs to be an area in which negotiation is possible. This can be created by having a very clear idea of what the best outcome would be and what the least favourable, but tolerable, outcome would be. The third pillar in this process is what happens if there is no agreement. For example, for the purchaser, is there an alternative product, or is the product only a 'nice to have'? There are three simple acronyms for these key negotiation parameters:

MFP = Most Favoured Position.[2] This equals the best possible outcome. For the purchaser this might equal no price increase and a few extra end-users. For the publisher or salesperson this might equal the full asking price plus the agreement to subscribe to another product.

WAP = Walk Away Position. This equals the least favourable outcome, but one which could be tolerated. For example, for the purchaser this might be a small amount over the budgeted price and access to remain for core users. For the publisher or salesperson this might equal a zero price increase and an agreement for information to be disseminated outside the organization at no extra cost.

BATNA = Best Alternative to a Negotiated Agreement.[3] This is the 'what if?' scenario. What if no agreement can be reached? The conclusion by the purchaser might be that agreement must be reached as the product is so important to their organization. This therefore affects what their WAP would be, as the imperative to get an agreement means they may need to accept terms that are less favourable if that is the only option. On a more positive note, a BATNA might be an awareness of an alternative product which, while it would be logistically painful for an organization to change over, would be a possibility, and means that whilst the WAP would still be quite unfavourable, it would be better than if coming to an agreement were the only option.

Seeing this diagrammatically can show where the common ground lies (see Figure 1.2). However, Figure 1.2 is quite rudimentary as it focuses on the issue of price, which is rarely the sole ground for negotiation. In addition, the maximum that a purchaser is willing to pay is rarely revealed to the publisher so the figure shows that negotiation is about finding that common ground.

Purchaser	Price	Publisher
MFP = £1000 and extra user access	£1000	
		WAP = £1100 and like-for-like renewal
Common ground between £1100 and £1300 is where negotiation lies, with some discussion on other issues, such as the number of users or level of access		
WAP = £1300 and continuation of core access		
	£1500	MFP = £1500 and extra user access

Figure 1.2   Finding the common ground in a negotation

The above can also be summarized by Kenny Rogers' words in his song 'The Gambler': *'You gotta know when to hold 'em, know when to fold 'em, know when to walk away and know when to run.'*

Arriving at these criteria is not usually a difficult thing to achieve; starting points include what you can afford to pay, what was paid before and what value it will add to the organization. If a more complicated and key negotiation is anticipated, then it may benefit from a small brainstorming exercise. A successful brainstorming consists of:

- a clear goal
- a number of participants: not too many, but again not too few, usually between four and eight. If there are larger groups, these may be best

broken down into smaller groups to focus on different issues in turn
- a format that differentiates it from the participants' usual meetings or discussions
- a facilitator: someone to keep the meeting on target, to ask questions and to jump start or suggest ideas if at first none are forthcoming.

Having the three criteria of MFP, WAP and BATNA in mind at the negotiation means that the negotiator does not have too much to remember and any written notes need not be referred to. It is surprising how many people can read figures upside down when at the negotiating table!

Summary

All parties in the process need to have done sufficient preparation to determine their most desired outcome as well as their walk away position. These parameters are not just about price, but will include contract length, level of access and other features.

Summary of questions for the negotiator of the subscribing organization to answer prior to any contract negotiation:

- What are the budgetary parameters?
- Are there any business plans that might affect any decisions (e.g. change in government policies, new subjects being covered, expansion or reduction in workforce that might affect the number of users, merger with another firm, department or institution)?
- Is the organization obliged to tender for contracts over a certain value?
- Is there an arrangement with an agent to deal with contract or renewal queries (e.g. e-journals)?
- How does this information need to be used?
  — Does it need to be disseminated outside the organization?
  — What is the preferred format?
  — Does the information need to be reproduced (e.g in student packs or client briefings)?
- How does the information need to be accessed?
  — Does it need to use silent authentication, passwords or other means of security access?
  — Does the information need to be accessed from different locations?

- — Is there a need for a special interface?
- — Is there a need for it to searchable by third-party software?
- Who are the key users of the product and can they provide any feedback?
- Who are the beneficiaries of the information? A user may not be the same person as those who will benefit (e.g. in a law firm the user may be a trainee solicitor using it on behalf of a Partner who is using it to advise a client).
- Are there any reasons why the product should not have an extended subscription (e.g. three years)?
- How important is the product to the objectives of the organization? Can the organization manage without the product?
- If the product were not subscribed to, what would the consequences be?
- Who are the users?
  - — Numbers of users?
  - — Groups or types of user?
- Are there any other known relationships within the organization with the publisher (e.g. sponsorship by the publisher, advertising within the product by the organization, contracts for the same product at other locations of the organization)?

References

1   A summary of the tender values can be found at http://ted.publications.eu.int, going to 'about this site', or in the following directives: Directive 93/36, Directive 93/37, Directive 93/38 and Directive 92/50.

2   MFP and WAP are concepts of Michael Taylor Associates, Management Consultant, The Oast House, Horsegrove Farm, Rotherfield, East Sussex TN6 3LU.

3   Fisher, R. and Ury, W. (1999) *Getting to Yes: negotiating an agreement without giving in*, 2nd edn, London, Random House.

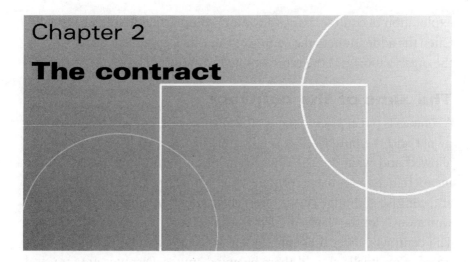

Chapter 2
The contract

This chapter cannot offer legal advice or interpretation as the author is not a lawyer.

The purpose of this chapter is to make the subscribing negotiator feel more comfortable about the contract, to examine what are the key sections of the contract and to explain some of the jargon. It also aims to emphasize that money is only one aspect of the negotiation process. It may also prove useful to a publisher or representative who is familiar with sales but new to dealing with contracts for electronic resources.

Depending on the size of the publisher, they may have their own in-house legal team to draft the contract. Some smaller publishers may have paid an outside firm to compile the contract. Being aware of this can help the subscribing organization understand how easy it would be for the publisher to amend the terms of the contract if that were what was needed. Some organizations prefer to use standard contracts for all their products, ranging from software and outsourced cleaning contracts to plant maintenance and online subscriptions.

Often the contract does not need any alterations to suit the particular needs of the subscribing organization, but sometimes a few tweaks are desirable, if only to seek clarification. There is no need to make the exploration of contract issues any more complicated than it needs to be. Often the addendum to the contract of an e-mail communication between the organization and the representative is sufficient.

The aims of the contract

A contract is put in place to protect the interests of the publisher, the content owner and the purchaser. It is a document that clearly sets out what is allowed and what are the obligations of all parties concerned. To the inexperienced negotiator contracts might appear to be designed to baffle and confuse, although this is rarely their intention. Some contracts have won awards for the clarity of their wording; unfortunately many have not. The contract is a legal document and it usually mentions under which jurisdiction it falls should there be any disputes. Disputes are rare, and by ironing out any queries, misunderstandings or poor drafting, disputes will be highly unlikely.

The contract as a key part of the preparation process

The number of organizations that never read the contract aligned to their online subscription is quite scary. The author conducted a mini poll in some workshop sessions that she did on the subject and found that on average between a half and one-third of delegates never read the contract that was being signed. The emphasis in negotiation can all too often be on the price, but it is the terms of the contract that tell the organization how they are permitted to use the product and what their obligations are. Reading the contract is a key part of the preparation process.

For major subscriptions the contract is still usually in paper format and is formally signed by the subscribing organization and usually the publisher too. For smaller subscriptions, especially single-user licences, it is often possible to just click on an electronic box saying 'I have read and accept the terms and conditions' and then buy the product online.

After reading the contract it may become apparent that the information cannot be used in the way intended. For example, dissemination of the information may be excluded. How the information can be used and by whom can severely affect the value of the product to the organization. The negotiator needs to identify areas that must be changed or which are desirable to be changed before the negotiation can be concluded.

We explored the key concepts of MFP (Most Favoured Position) and WAP (Walk Away Position) near the end of the previous chapter. Looking at the terms of the contract will define some of the organization's basic negotiation points, its WAP. Typical examples of deal breakers might include:

- amending the dissemination permissions
- amending the definition of a user
- changing the termination clause
- extending the use of the product to users who are temporarily off-site (e.g. on student exchange years or cross-border work)
- securing options to gets refunds or to cancel the contract if significant content is removed.

If the above criteria are not critical to forming an agreement, they may well be only desirable changes and may form part of the MFP.

It is usual to sign a contract every year, or to sign a contract for an agreed period of time. If renewing a contract, the assumption is that the contract remains the same as the previous term. However, especially if changes were made to the publisher's standard contract in previous negotiations, it is essential to re-read the contract each subscription term just in case the amendments have not been carried over into the new subscription period or the contract has materially changed.

Who should read the contract?

Each subscribing organization will have its own procedures about who gets involved in contracts. It may be that the subscribing negotiator does not need to defer to anyone else. The person who signs the contract may well differ from the person who negotiates it. Others who may get involved, especially if they differ from who does the negotiation, are in-house lawyers, procurement specialists, information professionals and end-users. If passing the contract on to someone else to read, it needs to be made clear what information needs to be gleaned. Typical questions will include:

From negotiator to end-user:
- Do the terms of the contract allow you to use the product as you would wish?

From negotiator to in-house lawyer or procurement specialist:
- I want to be able to do 'x' – does this contract permit us to do so?
- Are there any terms in here which you consider unfair?

Key sections of the contract

A contract may consist of more than one part. For example, there may be a section called the 'terms of service' which forms the bulk of the contract. Aligned to the terms of service there may be a document containing information about the subscription which is more relevant to the subscribing organization. This might be called something like 'subscription agreement'. The subscription agreement usually contains information about what elements of the product are subscribed to, the subscription term and the price. It is essential to check that if a part of a contract refers to another part, all parts are included. In some instances the main part of the contract does not change upon renewal, only the subscription agreement.

Many contracts follow a similar structure, containing key elements. While the entire contract does need to be read, of course, there are sections that do not need to concern you too much, such as the legal jargon about liabilities should you trip over and fall while reading the contract or making decisions based on the information supplied. Some contracts are well structured and have clear headings for each of the major parts, making it easier to check a particular piece of information.

Definitions

A contract often starts with definitions. It may be that this section is missed out altogether, either because the contract is beautifully brief, or because it is so clear throughout that definitions are not needed. Where definitions are spelled out at some point in the contract, typically they include:

- the user or subscriber – clarifying who is allowed access and at what locations. If the negotiator is aware that the organization might be changing name or format (e.g. in a merger), then this might need to be discussed as part of the negotiation.
- subscription period or authorized period – from when until when the contract period runs. Sometimes the authorized period will refer to the fact that content can continue to be used past a subscription period but is no longer updated.
- the product/service/information – defining what is being subscribed to. Sometimes this refers to an appendix if the product is modular.

Where there are definitions these are usually made to stand out throughout the contract via the use of either a capital letter at the start of the word, italics or emboldening.

Term or length

If information about the length of the contract is not included in a definitions section, it is usually found either in a subscription agreement prior to the main terms of the contract or fairly early on in the contract. The contract may have been agreed for more than the usual single year. If it is not mentioned, it needs to be ensured that it is clear when payment is due. It could be catastrophic for an organization to sign a three-year deal intending to pay annually, only to find that they are under an obligation to pay all three years up front.

The term or length of the contract is a key negotiation point. If the publisher can be guaranteed revenue for a number of years, this has a certain value that might be reflected in a lower price or a smaller increase in price. The purchaser has to weigh up a commitment for a number of years with the possibility of alternative products coming on to the market, ensuring continued good service and internal budget requirements. From an administrative point of view, knowing what is going to be paid in future years makes budget planning for both sides far easier and means that time-consuming negotiations do not need to be held every year.

Cancellation

This section might be called cancellation or 'term and termination'. It is often in the same section as the term or length part of the contract. It will outline what procedures need to be followed should the subscriber decide to cease subscribing to the product. It also describes the circumstances and terms under which the publisher might terminate the contract. It is essential to ensure that the contract is not weighted too much in favour of one party.

There may be a clause in this section requiring the subscriber to notify the publisher a certain time in advance of the end of the subscription if they wish to cancel. Typically this notification period is anything between 30 and 90 days. If the contract is being really pedantic, the notification period may also refer to the inability to notify of an intention to cancel prior to a certain date, resulting in a window of typically just 30 days if the subscriber wishes to cancel. At the other end of the spectrum there may be no requirement to notify the publisher of any intention to cancel.

It is necessary to keep track of the notification periods to avoid being in a poor position at the negotiation stage. A variety of tools can be used to achieve this, ranging from a spreadsheet to diary reminders and online catalogues. It is up to each organization to decide how they wish to manage the requirement by the publisher to notify them of any intention to cancel. Options include: only notifying the publisher if there is a true intention to cancel, writing letters as standard reserving the right to cancel, or a combination of the two depending on the value of the product. The advantages to the subscriber of writing a letter reserving the right to cancel include the following:

- It places the obligation on the publisher to contact the purchaser nearer the renewal time.
- If financial cuts need to be made by an organization, then they have greater choice of what to cancel if they are within what would otherwise be a period when they are obliged to renew.

- If a new product comes on the market within the notification period, then this can be taken into the negotiation equation.
- It provides reassurance to superiors that the negotiator is managing their subscriptions well and with flexibility in mind.
- It makes the negotiator appear assertive.
- If the timetable for renewal discussions gets close to the renewal date, then pressure is removed.
- The purchaser is in a stronger position nearer the renewal date as they are not obliged to renew, meaning that their WAP is potentially to subscribe to an alternative or to truly cancel the product.

A letter reserving the right to cancel is therefore a polite way of informing the publisher that the subscriber wishes to keep their options open. The legal phrase for this 'keeping your options open' is 'without prejudice'. It is not advisable to use legal jargon in a letter unless absolutely confident about what it means. There is the chance that if no subsequent communication takes place between subscriber and publisher following the writing of such a letter, then the subscription will automatically cease. However, publishers rarely let this happen, and nor do well organized librarians. Depending on any restrictions in the contract, when to write these letters is again the choice of the purchaser. The letters can even be written at the same time as the renewal so that it does not become a separate administrative process. Sample clauses that might be contained within such a letter are shown in Figure 2.1.

Some contracts contain quite punitive clauses for failure to renew or for failure to negotiate renewal terms in advance. Examples include an automatic increase in the price or a severance fee. Fortunately these instances are rare, but the fact that they exist in some contracts mean that the negotiator needs to remain vigilant.

Start with 'nice' introduction or refer to something recent.
For example: 'It was good to have the opportunity to meet recently and confirm the renewal of our subscription to XXX.'

Do the 'practical'/formal part
For example:
(a) Without prejudice please treat this letter as notification of our intention to cancel our subscription to XXX at the end of our current term, as required under clause 10.2 of our subscription agreement (two months in advance by registered letter).

Or

(b) As required under clause 5 of our contract, we notify you of our intention to cancel our subscription to the three online sources previously mentioned.

Finish on a positive note
For example:
(a) However, we do look forward to discussing the renewal of XXX nearer to the time of our subscription end.

Or

(b) . . . but without prejudice should we find that the usage statistics advise us otherwise.

Figure 2.1　　Sample clauses for 'without prejudice' letters

✓　　To summarize the key points about cancellation for negotiation purposes, be clear about the following:

- If the publisher ceases the subscription, and where the subscriber has not been at fault, then the subscriber should be entitled to a proportional refund of any up-front cost.
- If the organization does wish to cancel the product, by what date does it have to notify the publisher?
- The organization needs to decide if it is necessary to write a letter reserving its right to cancel the product.
- Whether there are any cancellation terms that the organization wishes to amend.

Limitations and permissions

Each contract lays out what the user is and is not allowed to do with the information that it has subscribed to. It will also explain how the information might, or might not, be used by those to whom the end-user intends to give it. It is key to ensure that the permissions outlined in the contract match the needs of the organization. Where there are significant limitations, then the value of the product to the organization will be affected and this needs to be explained in the negotiation phase. For example, some information may be embargoed in a particular jurisdiction. Being aware if the information is owned by the publisher or is third-party information will usually affect the chances of permissions being extended beyond what is allowed in the standard contract. Where the product is an aggregation of a variety of sources it may be virtually impossible for the publisher to liaise with all the content owners to obtain a contract amendment that is requested by just one organization.

> ✓ To summarize this section on limitations and permissions, be clear about the following:
>
> - Where can the product be used (i.e. can it be used off-site)?
> - How can the information be used (e.g. can it be disseminated or used in packs of materials)?
> - Who has access?

Liabilities and obligations

Cost

Liabilities include the cost to the organization of using the database and penalties for the misuse of the product. The cost most usually appears in the subscription agreement section of the contract. Where costs are mentioned in the main part of the contract it may just refer to them as something like 'price agreed'. Other places where the price might be included are the order document, an invoice or a schedule/appendix of agreed cost. Ensure that the mention of cost is clear about when payment is due. This is especially important in multi-year deals. It is also important to check if there is any specification of how the cost should be paid, for example yearly in advance, monthly by direct debit. For smaller organizations or sole traders the ability to pay monthly might seriously help with cash-flow issues and therefore be an ideal point on which to negotiate. For the publisher a monthly payment may not be quite so attractive but can mean that revenues stay the same (despite a small loss of interest) and it is an easy option to offer without really compromising – one example of where both publisher and purchaser can win without either side losing out.

Confidentiality clauses

Some contracts preclude the subscriber from discussing the price outside their organization. This is not usually a deal-breaking problem but may be something that is amended by the subscriber should they feel strongly about being able to compare prices paid. As an example, some consortium licences, such as Eduserv in the UK, publish not only the text of the contract but the agreed price in the list of their agreements.[1] Other confidentiality issues might include a restriction on showing the product to parties outside the organization, even where content is not passed on. These confidentiality terms are designed to protect the publisher from competitors viewing their product and gleaning ideas for improving their own products. A subscribing organization might wish to have a confidentiality clause put into their contract to protect their data and any information about the organization that might be gained from various sources, ranging from meetings to usage data. Confidentiality clauses can stand on their own outside a contract, and it is not unusual for a publisher to sign a confidentiality clause when working on a particular project for the subscribing organization, for example in setting up automated searches on matters which the subscriber wishes to keep out of the public domain.

Jurisdiction

It is only necessary to worry about the jurisdiction of the contract if the country or state given is not instantly recognizable and might fall into the category, for example, of an offshore jurisdiction, where laws may be less transparent and might offer less protection. However, where the invoice originates may affect an organization that has to pay tax on the service. For example, in the UK a business can reclaim value added tax, which is charged at 17.5%, whereas other types of organization often cannot reclaim the VAT. Some international publishers can choose from where they issue their invoices and the tax put on the product in that country may be more favourable to the subscribing organization. This is another example of where both publisher and purchaser can gain without either losing out.

Obligations

An obligation might include an onus being placed upon the subscriber to ensure that end-users are apprised of any restrictions on the use of the information. Some publishers put in their contracts that there is an obligation to actively promote the product within the subscribers' organization, either via training or by other forms of awareness-raising sessions. It is up to the information professional to decide how this might be conveyed to interested parties within the organization. It might be part of the training process, it might form part of their induction to the organization, it might be appended to the end of an e-mail when the information professional sends any data from that product to anyone else. If there are numerous obligations or administrative tasks required, this may be another area that affects the value of the product to the organization. The negotiator therefore needs to note these liabilities and judge whether they are likely to have a significant impact and need to be raised as part of the negotiation.

The obligations of the publisher usually entail them making 'fair and reasonable' efforts to ensure that the correct information is delivered in a timely fashion to the subscriber. There is usually a very wordy section limiting their liability should the subscriber use their information, rely on it and as a result lose out. Where a subscribing organization passes on costs incurred, for example on a pay-as-you-go basis, a failure of the financial reporting tool of the product might turn out to be extremely costly to them. It is worth the subscribing organization clarifying the liability of the publisher should something like this happen. Where access, reliability and accuracy are key, the possibility of a separate service level agreement may be another negotiating point.

To summarize this section, when determining any liabilities or obligations that need to be part of the negotiation, be clear about the following:

- Do end-users need to be informed about how they are allowed to use the information (e.g. where there is an obligation on the organization to make all reasonable efforts to ensure they do not send the information to people outside the organization)?
- If the price is mentioned, does this match the amount you expect to pay as well as how it will be paid and when?
- Are there any obligations that are onerous and would devalue the product?
- Are the liabilities to the organization clear and fair? For example, make sure that the organization is not obliged to pay for a product under all circumstances, such as if the product is terminated or if a key component of the product is removed.
- What are the liabilities to the organization if they breach any of these obligations?
- Does it matter from which country the invoice is issued for the purposes of tax?

Below is an example of a rather wordy contract. It is purely fictitious. This example consists of two sections: one is the subscription agreement, the other is the terms of service. The wording is particularly controversial in some places to highlight some of the issues that can arise. Fortunately most contracts will not need much, if any, amendment. The sample contract has been marked up where it might be desirable to make amendments or seek clarification. As previously mentioned, it is not always necessary to change the text of the contract: sometimes an e-mail from the representative may be sufficient.

This example is of a contract where the cost is based on pay-as-you-go rates, but by paying in advance a discount or certain amount of 'free' data is given.

Bloggs Data Ltd
Pre-payment agreement for
Christmas-Carols-R-Us Ltd

30 September 2005

Bloggs Data Ltd
A Building • 100 A Street • London EC1X 1AA
T +44 (0)20 7000 4000 • F +44 (0)20 7000 4000
www.bloggsdata.co.uk

CONTACT DETAILS			
Company:	Christmas-Carols-R-Us Ltd		
Principal Contact:	Fiona Durrant		
Job Title:	Library & Information Centre Manager		
Department:	Knowledge Management		
Address:	100 North Pole Street		
City:	London	Postcode:	EC7 1YY
Country:	England		
E-mail:	fiona.durrant@christmascarols.com		
Tel:	0207 919 1858	Fax:	0207 919 1999

PRODUCT REQUIREMENTS	Number of Users	Amount £
News service	5	
Swedish cases	5	
Bloggs roundup	5	
Total to be invoiced		£3000
Free advance payment quota @10%		£300
TOTAL usage available including free quota		**£3300**

What provisions are there for when you use this amount up prior to the end of the contract term? If you don't spend all this money what provisions are there?

Bloggs Data will issue an invoice which should be settled within 30 days

SERVICE PERIOD	
Start Date	2 January 2006
End Date	29 December 2006

Why isn't this a full year? 2 January 2006 is a Monday. 1 Jan when it should renew is a public holiday, 29 Dec is first day that is not a weekend or public holiday. Some publishers' computers cannot renew at weekends and automatically default to the day before the subscription started.

Insert some wording here to protect yourself and prevent invoices being issued months in advance.

This Pre-payment agreement is made in conjunction with the separate Terms of Service. The signatures below are agreeing to both the Pre-payment agreement and the terms of service.

CLIENT	BLOGGS DATA
Signature:	Signature:
Name:	Name:
Date:	Date:

Ensure you get to keep on file a signed copy of the contract.

BLOGGS DATA

TERMS OF SERVICE

BLOGGS DATA (BD) PROVIDES THE SERVICE AND INFORMATION TO YOU SUBJECT TO THE FOLLOWING TERMS OF SERVICE (TOS) IN CONJUNCTION WITH THE PRE-PAYMENT AGREEMENT YOU HAVE EXECUTED.

BD may amend these TOS from time to time by updating this page on their client extranet. Your continued use of the Site after revisions have been made will indicate your acceptance of the revised TOS.

1. The following terms shall have the following definitions:

    Agreement: Your Pre-payment agreement together with these TOS and any documents referred to in them to the exclusion of all other terms;

    Authorized Period: The period during which BD shall provide you with access to the Service, as outlined in the Pre-payment agreement.

    BD: Bloggs Data or Bloggs Data Limited, as set out in the Pre-payment agreement;

    Database(s): Any or all of the BD modules, being a collection of independent works, data or other materials arranged and/or collated by BD in a systematic or methodical way which you can access via the Service;

    Pre-payment agreement: The memorandum of certain terms and conditions signed by you and BD;

    Equipment: The computer system, including terminals, other hardware and software used to enable you to receive the Bloggs Data Service;

    Free quota: The amount of usage available once pre-payment amount has been used up. This is only available on advance payment of sums of £2000 or more;

    Information: Any item of information contained in a BD Database;

    Intellectual Property Rights: Copyright, database rights, trade marks, goodwill and other intellectual property or similar rights;

    Service: The information service provided by BD.

Get them to agree to inform you of changes.

Here you might refer to any specially negotiated terms that appear later in the contract.

If necessary refer to a service level agreement here.

Get a definition of who you are, plus a definition of a user.

2.   The Service
You shall be responsible for providing, and for all
communications charges and costs associated with, the
Equipment.

You acknowledge that the Information does not constitute
investment advice or an offer to sell or the solicitation of an
offer to buy any security of any enterprise in any jurisdiction.
You hereby represent, warrant and agree (a) that to the
extent that the Information relates to any securities offerings
to which reference is made above, you will not use any of
such Information or the Service for the purpose of offering or
selling, or soliciting any offer to purchase, any security (or
for the purpose of assisting, directly or indirectly, or
participating, directly or indirectly, in any such undertaking)
to or from any person or in any circumstance that would
violate such restrictions or the securities or other laws of
any jurisdiction and (b) not to disseminate by any means
any material obtained from the database or any person or
entity outside your own organization.

Qualify this so that it is subject to any permissions granted in the sections below.

You agree to defend, indemnify and hold harmless BD from
any breach of the obligations, representations and
warranties contained in this Section 2.

Clause to inform you of changes.

BD reserves the right to change the price of
Information as outlined in Appendix I from
time to time.

Check that appendix is included.

3.   BD's Grant of Rights and Your Acknowledgment of
Limitations
BD grants to you a non-exclusive and non-transferrable
licence to access the Service and to use the Information for
the Authorized Period subject to the terms of this
Agreement. You may not sub-license these rights in any
manner, or enter into any arrangement that would have the
effect of sub-licensing the rights granted herein.
You acknowledge that in using the Service, you do not
acquire any Intellectual Property Rights or right, title or

What does non-transferrable mean if you merge or the organization changes name? See definitions.

the Service except the right to use the Service as set forth in this Agreement.

You agree that the Information will not be reproduced, revealed, or made available to anyone else, it being understood that the Information is licensed for your internal use only. No information belonging to BD may be circulated by you in the United States of America. You agree to indemnify, defend, and hold harmless BD from any claim or cause of action against BD arising out of or relating to use of the Information by individuals or entities which have not been authorized by this Agreement to have access to and/or use the Information.

If BD becomes aware that any of the Information is copied, used or disclosed otherwise than as permitted by this Agreement then you agree to promptly take such steps as BD may request (including the institution of legal proceedings to remedy the default if capable of remedy) and/or to prevent any other unauthorized copying, disclosure or use. BD's remedies under this section are without prejudice to any other remedy BD may have at law or equity.

You agree (a) only to use the Service during the Authorized Period and in the course of your customary in-house research and other in-house activities; (b) not to reproduce Information other than when downloading and viewing the same on the Equipment or on physical copies printed out at your premises, for your internal use only and not for any commercial exploitation; (c) not to permit the Service to be made available on a network, or otherwise transmitted, broadcast or displayed without the prior written permission of the BD; (d) not to distribute or sell or make available to any third party, in whole or part, either directly or indirectly any part of the Information or elements of the Service without the prior written consent of BD; (e) not to use the Service and the Information to develop or provide, directly or indirectly, a product or service that is competitive with the services provided by BD; (f) not to alter or modify the

If dissemination is required you will need to insert a clause permitting you to pass on small amounts of information to third parties and refer to this in other parts of the contract.

Do the restrictions (e.g. cannot circulate in the USA), affect how you want to use the information? See if contract refers to any penalties if you do breach terms.

Information or elements of the Service in any way and to inform those to whom you disseminate the information of this obligation (g) not to use the Service other than in accordance with applicable UK legislation.

The software provided by BD as part of the Service is and remains the property of BD or its licensors, and shall not be modified, disassembled, reverse engineered or transferred.

Except as where otherwise indicated, all trade marks included within the Service, expressly including 'Bloggs Data', are the property of BD. BD reserves all rights in its trade marks.

4. Term and Termination
The term of the Agreement is contemporaneous with the Authorized Period, unless terminated earlier, as provided in this Agreement.

BD may terminate this Agreement at any time and for any reason without notice, and shall have no liability to you whatsoever. Upon such termination, you shall remain responsible for all past due amounts you owe to BD, if any.

Notification of termination by the user must be received by BD at least 30 days prior to the end of the term of the current Agreement. If notification is not received then renewal for a further term will commence with the assumption that the amount owing to BD will be the amount paid by the user in the previous term plus 25%.

5. Limitation of Liability
You acknowledge that the service and information are provided on an 'as is' basis, and that BD does not make any representations or warranties to the timeliness, currency, accuracy, completeness, merchantability, or fitness for a particular purpose. You also acknowledge that every business decision involves the assumption of a risk and that BD, in providing the information to you, does not and will not

This clause is heavily weighted in favour of the publisher.

Clause here entitling you to money back if prices rise beyond a certain point.

Clause here about refunding unused money within so many days.

This clause is very punitive towards the subscriber: at least the second sentence should be struck out.

Fairly standard clause protecting publisher from liability.

be liable in any manner whatsoever. You therefore agree that BD will not be liable for any loss, damage or injury caused in whole or in part by BD's negligence or recklessness in obtaining, delivering, collecting, interpreting, reporting, or communicating the information. You agree that BD will never be liable for direct or indirect or lost profits damages, even if advised of their possibility.

Notwithstanding the above, BD does not seek to exclude or limit liability for death or personal injury resulting from its own negligence or any other liability the exclusion or limitation of which is expressly prohibited by law.

You shall indemnify BD and its licensors against claims, demands, costs, losses and expenses incurred by BD as a result of or arising out of your breach of any representation, warranty or agreement contained herein or from the unauthorized use of the user passwords or the Service.

6. Miscellaneous
    You shall not assign, transfer, create any trust over, charge or deal in any other manner with all or any part of this Agreement or grant, declare, create or dispose of any right or interest therein without the prior written consent of BD.

The wording here is putting more onus on BD for failures owing to lack of care, although clauses about failures beyond the publishers' control are common.

You agree that BD shall not be liable for any failure delay or omission by it in the performance of its obligations under this Agreement if such failure delay or omission arises from any cause.

This sentence implies that amendments to the terms of the contract are made in the first part of the contract.

Nothing contained in this Agreement shall be for the benefit of any third parties unless expressly set forth in an applicable Pre-payment agreement. Unless otherwise set out in the Pre-payment agreement, this Agreement shall be governed by and construed in all respects in accordance with the laws of England. Subject to the Pre-payment agreement, you agree that in the event of any dispute arising from this Agreement that cannot be resolved by good faith negotiation you will submit to the non-exclusive jurisdiction of the English courts. In the event that any dispute becomes the subject of litigation, the prevailing party shall be entitled to an award of its actual costs and legal fees.

No failure or delay by BD in exercising its rights under this Agreement will operate as a waiver of that right nor will any single or partial exercise by BD of any right preclude any further exercise of any other right.

APPENDIX I
Prices of documents

News service	
Headline	No charge
Headline and search in context	£1
Full text article	£3
Swedish cases	
Casename	No charge
Headnote	£3
Judgement	£5
Proceedings	£5
Bloggs roundup	
Headline	No charge
Report	£5

Issues more related to a service level agreement or to add weight to an argument to get more 'free' quota might include how good is the reporting module. For example, can you get a usage statement that you can send to your accounts department?

Standard contracts

Some organizations prefer to have standard wording for all their contracts. This can prove problematic for the specific requirements that online resources usually have, so the most common approach is to have a standard contract specifically for all online resources. It would be virtually impossible for a standard contract to be any use were it the same for the outsourced cleaning staff as well as the subscription to a collection of newspapers online. A standard contract may also be the main basis or starting point for a specific licence, with the parties making a few tweaks depending on the product, purchaser and publisher.

One example where consortium-led standard terms exist is in the UK education sector, where the majority of online products will be purchased under standard contracts made by JISC/NESLI or Eduserv/CHEST.[2] Most students will know these resources by the point of access generic term of 'Athens'. CHEST maintains a list of what it calls 'datasets', for which it has negotiated an agreement.[3] It is then possible for academic-sector non-participants to look at the agreements and choose whether they wish to opt in, usually subject to a payment. These licences were drafted to reflect the specific requirements of the sector while recognizing the interests of the publisher. The standard Eduserv licence covers usage for the normal business of a university, taken to include 'teaching; research; personal educational development; administration and the management of the Licensee's organization; development work associated with any of the above'. Specifically excluded are 'consultancy or services leading to commercial exploitation of the product; work of significant benefit to the employer of students on industrial placement or part-time courses'. Generally, off-site access, whether by distance learners or others, is permitted. However, use by retired members of staff, alumni and the employers of part-time students is not allowed.[4]

The Joint Information Systems Committee (JISC) plays a similar role to that of Eduserv.[5] JISC currently has three model licences which represent the subtle differences between types of online resource. These three licences are for Datasets, eBooks and electronic journals, the latter being specifically looked after by NESLI. NESLI is the UK's national initiative for the licensing of electronic journals on behalf of the higher and further education and research communities.

There may be reference within either a standard or a non-standard contract to an industry-wide standard code of practice. One example of this is the international body COUNTER, the Counting Online Usage of NeTworked Electronic Resources.[6] COUNTER's aims are to facilitate the recording and exchange of online usage statistics and claim that their standards provide benefits to both publisher and subscriber alike.

In agreement with the publisher, some organizations are known to append their standard wording to the product's own contract with the qualification that where there may be contradictions, the organization's own wording is taken as the version that is correct. The advantage of standard wording is that it is not necessary to consult lots of different contracts to check common details, for example when the notification period falls.

Summary

The contract and the terms it contains is fertile ground for negotiation. The contract may not suit the exact needs of the subscribing organization and some amendments may be easy and free to make, whereas some may have value and require more robust discussions.

> ✓ To summarize what needs to be done with the contract be clear about the following:
>
> - Is there a standard contract that needs to be used?
> - Read the contract. Who else in your organization needs to read and/or approve it?
>   — What are you being given access to?
>   — How can the material be disseminated?
>   — Who has access?
>   — What does it cost? (both upfront and any other ongoing costs)
>   — Until when are you committed?
>   — What are the renewal dates?
>   — Is there a termination clause?
> - Clarify with the publisher any terms you do not understand.
> - Are any terms unfavourable or prevent you from using the product how you wish?

> ✓
> - Are you able to change contract terms?
> - Are there any actions you need to take, such as writing a letter reserving your right to cancel or informing users of limitations or cost (using various methods such as automatic pop-ups when a user clicks on a link, or a simple annual e-mail or awareness when training end-users)?

References

1 Eduserv/CHEST Datasets Agreements, www.eduserv.org.uk/chest/datasets/table-index.html [accessed August 2005].
2 www.eduserv.org.uk/chest/.
3 Eduserv/CHEST Datasets Agreements, www.eduserv.org.uk/chest/datasets/table-index.html.
4 Standard Eduserv agreement, www.eduserv.org.uk/chest/datasets-agreement.rtf.
5 JISC collections, www.jisc.ac.uk/collbrowse.html.
6 COUNTER Code of Practice for Journals and Databases (published April 2005), www.projectcounter.org/code_practice.html.

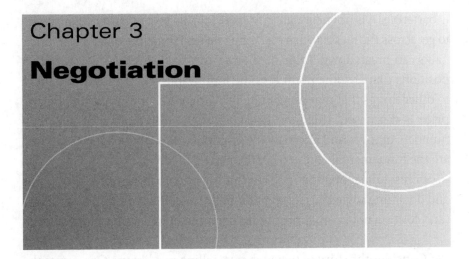

Chapter 3
Negotiation

The actual negotiation is the stage most feared by many representatives and information professionals alike. The aim of this book is to take away any fear and to provide confidence through examples, practical tips and more detailed analysis. In this chapter, the issues of how to broach the subject of the renewal, how to discuss money and terms and how to 'close the deal' are all explored. The negotiation can be done during any phase of the subscription. There may be reasons for holding a negotiation early, such as needing precise figures for a budget submission. It may be that a price is agreed well ahead of time, with confirmation about the renewal going ahead coming later. The ideal situation is one where neither party is feeling pressured by time so that they can concentrate on their real objectives.

The purpose of the negotiation is to serve your interests. The objective will have been decided as part of the preparation process. Before you enter negotiations, know your Most Favoured Position (MFP), Walk Away Position (WAP) and the Best Alternative to a Negotiated Agreement (BATNA).

Successful negotiation is not about one side stating their position, the other side moving a bit, then going back and forth in painful steps. This is slow, can damage the relationship between publisher and subscriber and involves the concept of 'giving in'. The most common example of this is bartering; it is not negotiation at its best. This sort of bartering manages to get across the message that one wants a cheap price, the other a high price. Talks can break down if this method is used exclusively, as it is based on positions that at some point become immovable and pays little attention to other things that may ameliorate the situation. For example, if only the price is discussed, this ignores issues such as frequency of payment, numbers of users and alternative subscription models. What gets ignored are the fundamental concerns of the parties involved.

Successful negotiation is about finding out what the other side wants and obtaining a winning solution for both sides. Roger Fisher gives a good (and for this book, an appropriate) example in his book *Getting to Yes*:

> Consider the story of two men quarrelling in a library. One wants the window open and the other wants it closed. They bicker back and forth about how much to leave it open; a crack, halfway, three-quarters of the way. No solution satisfies them both.
>
> Enter the librarian. She asks one why he wants the window open: 'To get some fresh air.' She asks the other why he wants it closed: 'To avoid the draft.' After thinking a minute, she opens wide a window in the next room, bringing in fresh air without a draft.[1]

The method of communication

There are different mechanisms which can be used to discuss a renewal. The most common are telephone, e-mail and face-to-face meetings. Other less commonly used methods might include video conferencing and letters or faxes. In reality a combination of methods is used to get to the final agreement. A favoured format is often to open negotiations with e-mails, have a meeting, and then to conclude again with e-mails or letters and a contract. The key advantages and disadvantages of the more commonly used methods are outlined below:

E-mail
- Quick
- Have a record of negotiations
- Cannot see body language

- Not ideal for complex negotiations
- Good for products that have low price and therefore less room for negotiation
- Can include others by forwarding e-mails without the knowledge of the sender.

Letter

- Administrative
- Have a record of the negotiations
- Cannot see body language
- Not ideal for complex negotiations
- Good for products that have a low price and therefore less room for negotiation
- Very formal.

Meetings

- Face to face
- Can see body language
- Builds up a relationship with the representative
- Can feel under pressure to achieve a solution in one sitting
- Can take longer, especially if it involves more than one meeting.

Telephone

- Can hear inflections in voice
- Cannot see body language
- Builds up a relationship with the representative
- Can be quick
- Not automatically recorded.

In more complex negotiations it is useful to be able to refer to a log of communications and outstanding issues. This means that if a point is queried, you know where to look to verify that information. A log might consist of just line entries in date or subject order, scored through once the issue has been solved satisfactorily. It is useful to keep the entries on the log rather than delete them once an issue has been resolved, just in case the same issue arises again. Figure 3.1 shows an example of such a log.

Product XYZ
5 Jan. 2006 wrote letter reserving right to cancel addressed to Rep, telephoned rep warning her to expect it.

~~Missing content~~
~~3 July 2006 Telephoned helpdesk about missing news content~~
~~5 July 2006 Received e-mail from rep saying she was looking into missing content issue~~
~~13 July 2006 Chased via e-mail status of missing content~~
~~14 July 2006 Rep telephoned to say content had been restored, checked to verify this correct and it had been restored~~

Meetings
15 Aug. 2006 E-mailed rep asking for convenient dates for renewal meeting, agreed 11am 12 Sept. at our offices.

Figure 3.1   Example of a log tracking negotiations

Such information can easily be stored in the library catalogue, within a dedicated file on the publisher or product, or on a spreadsheet of information kept about online subscriptions. It can be as simple as a column in a spreadsheet called 'letter reserving right to cancel' and entering in the date or saying 'not required'.

It is up to the negotiator to decide whether the issue of price is kept separate from discussions on changing contract terms or gaining extra privileges. However, price and terms are usually wrapped up in one another. Where there seems to be little movement on the price, then, for example, the addition of extra access to the product may be pursued more vigorously.

Bi-party, consortium and multi-party negotiations
Bi-party negotiations
The type of organization will affect whether that organization is more commonly dealing in bi-party negotiation or multi-party deals. Bi-party

negotiations involve just the two sides, the purchaser and the vendor, and each is able to make decisions without referring to another party.

Consortium negotiations

Often academic institutions are part of a consortium where a nominated body or institution is given authority to negotiate on all their behalves, without then having to refer back to the many individual subscribing organizations. The purpose of a consortium from the point of view of the members is to have power in numbers and therefore to get the best price and terms. For the publisher, a consortium offers one point of contact and the concessions they make may be balanced by the amount of time and money they save by only dealing with one body. However, where there is an intermediary, such as a consortium, there is a danger that the direct publisher–customer relationship for all participating subscribers may be lost. Some publishers may arrange for their representatives to maintain a direct relationship in spite of a consortium-led negotiation. If direct access to support services, representatives and account managers is desirable then this needs to be conveyed as part of the negotiation. For publishers, especially small companies or those new to the trade, it can be confusing to work out exactly who to contact in order to arrange a new agreement. There are many different types of consortium, ranging from organizations with similar interests in a particular geographical area to those which have a common purpose, such as universities.

Advantages and disadvantages of a consortium

For the publisher

+ One point of contact
+ Saves time and money dealing with one person
−/+ Weight of so many subscribers riding on a on a single agreement
− Less likely to be able to use own contract terms

For the purchaser

+ Power in numbers
+ Common interests
+ Expert does the negotiation
− Less flexibility
− Responsibility to do things not individually agreed

Consortia will draw up a document that outlines the main principles that concern them regarding the purchase of online resources. The consortium may choose to make this available publicly or it may decide to keep it as an internal document. Where so many organizations are involved, keeping such a document private may be quite difficult so they are not usually drafted with any contentious language and they do not name any particular publisher. Consortium agreements put an onus on both parties. For example, signed-up members may have an obligation to ensure that their technology is current enough to offer the end-users the latest and widest access, whereas a publisher may have to develop software to enable more complex logging of usage statistics. One example of a consortium agreement is the Statement of Current Perspective and Preferred Practices for the Selection and Purchase of Electronic Information by the International Coalition of Library Consortia.[2] In the UK academic sector, Eduserv/CHEST's principles are simple: 'CHEST negotiates for, and manages, agreements that users have asked for. It is driven only by demand and the need to provide better value for money than can be obtained elsewhere.'[3]

Multi-party negotiations

Multi-party deals involve a key negotiator communicating on behalf of a number of organizations, but they have to liaise backwards and forwards between the subscribing organizations and the publisher. The authority of the negotiator needs to be clarified with all parties at the outset and where referral needs to take place the mechanism and timescale for doing this need to be clearly planned. The goal to convey as many referrals as possible in one bundle rather than one at a time, which is annoying, time-consuming and hard to keep track of, should also be made clear. As so many issues go back and forth, multi-party deals benefit from having a specified note or minute taker, but a note taker may be present at any type of negotiation meeting.

There may be other dimensions or layers to all these types of deal, such as the finance director being the only person able to give a firm commitment, but the negotiation is being carried out by another individual.

Who to involve in the negotiation can become political. Some individuals may just need to be kept informed of developments, whereas others demand to be consulted. Many modern library electronic management systems can record who requested the product. If there is no electronic management system, then this information needs to be recorded in another way, ranging from a spreadsheet to a designated location in a note field. A key role for the information professional is to orchestrate the many people who might *want* (or not want) to be involved with those who *need* to be included. Too many people can slow the process down, while failing to involve a key person can completely stall the process at a late stage of the negotiation. It is surprising how the wrath of a person with a bruised ego can completely distract and hold to ransom a person trying to negotiate. An alternative policy is to agree with the interested parties who needs to be involved and to clarify what sort of information about the negotiation they wish to have passed on to them. The interested parties may just want confirmation of the renewal or to be consulted only if there is a serious consideration about ceasing the subscription.

Who might be involved in the negotiation?

- finance director
- information professional
- end-user
- information recipient
- person who chose product
- negotiator
- procurement specialist
- lawyer or contract signatory
- budget holder
- consortium convenor
- publisher
- representative
- salesperson
- IT department.

The problem of who to involve is often exacerbated by online publishers more frequently using automatic e-mails to inform end-users that their subscription is about to end. An information professional's nightmare is to discover that ten out of 20 end-users have followed the aforementioned e-mail instructions and renewed online, at full list price, with their credit cards and are now demanding that they be recompensed. A good publisher will sort out this predicament with the negotiator, but it does put the purchaser in a weaker negotiating position because the automatic renewal by ten individuals indicates that a high value is placed on the product by the end-users, meaning that the bulk discount might not be as high as they were expecting. Therefore, if in doubt, clarify with the publisher what sort of communication they send to end-users. If automatic e-mails cannot be switched off, then education of the end-user is the key. This also consolidates the position of the information professional, who needs to keep a good overview of what is going on. For the sole trader, all of this is wonderfully irrelevant as they will not need to consult with an array of other internal people.

The publisher and their products

The publisher is often portrayed as the money-hungry demon, but this is not always the case. The reputation of a publisher rests on the reliability, functionality and content of their product as well as their pricing structure and management of the customer relationship. The publisher has to make money in order to justify the existence of the product. Pricing is just one method of achieving this goal, but others include being stringent about usage of and access to their database.

The publisher will have a different perspective of their product from that of the purchaser. It is often the case that the publisher has been unable to see a competitor product in action. This has disadvantages for both parties as the publisher will not be able to explain to the purchaser why their product is the better option. If the subscriber wishes the publisher to better understand what they most like about a competitor product, and intends to achieve this by showing the publisher, they first need to refer to their contract for the competitor product and ensure that this is not prevented by a confidentiality clause. Knowing how much each party knows about a competitor product can only benefit each party in gaining a satisfactory outcome in the negotiation process.

Publishers may have signed up to codes of conduct or undertakings such as a clear English campaign or a professional organization's guidance on good publishing practice. A good publisher will not need to refer to the supporting documents, whereas the purchaser may find it useful to consult such documents if the situation gets to a difficult point.

Maintaining competition in the marketplace is in the interests of the subscriber and will benefit the product's development too.

Many sectors have experienced consolidation of the marketplace into a few key providers. This often creates problems of products either being withdrawn, absorbed into other, differently priced products, or just looking different. Publishers can even choose not to sell to a specific market if they feel that a competitor in that market has too strong a grip. Where a product is sold and there are concerns by users about how that might damage competition, it is up to the negotiator to make representations to a relevant body, either the competition authorities or a professional information organization. Competition is one certain way of keeping a publisher 'on its toes' in terms of price and functionality.

The relationship between publisher and purchaser

Every negotiator has a dual aspect to their dealings. First, they want to achieve their MFP as closely as possible, but they also have a sound reason to maintain a good working relationship with their counterpart. For example, the publisher negotiator wants to achieve a returning customer who feels happy enough to recommend their product, while the subscriber negotiator is interested in a relationship that will ensure good support and communication throughout the subscription term.

Different publishers manage their relationships with their subscribers in different ways. For small subscriptions that can be purchased electronically for small amounts of money, the relationship with the publisher is likely to remain an electronic one. For larger subscriptions, a representative is usually assigned to the purchasing company. Some publishers operate a more complex way of supporting their subscribers and may have an additional named telephone contact (as well as the representative) because the representative is often out of the office visiting subscribers.

Having a good relationship will assist you in seeing and appreciating the point of view of the other side. Being able to demonstrate that someone else's point of view is being genuinely considered will make them realize you are listening, and they are then more likely to listen seriously to the concerns you express. Trying to 'second guess' what the other side is thinking can help with exploring what their concerns might be, but too much and it will cloud the message that you are trying to get across.

Just like the subscriber, the publisher or representative will have their own goals to achieve in the negotiation process. They may also have internal negotiations. In the negotiation phase it is useful for each side to know who has the ultimate say about what is acceptable. For example, a representative needs to make it clear if they need to get authority for contract changes and how easy and quick that might be. The publisher needs to articulate well to the subscriber their reasons for pricing, access or other issues, and the subscriber has a responsibility to ask questions if these reasons are not clear to them.

A personal relationship often builds up between the publisher or representative and the subscriber. Sometimes there is a clash of personalities, and if it is really hindering the negotiations the subscriber should consider suggesting to the publisher that they deal with another person, tactfully explaining that it might not be due to poor service but due to different personalities and varied expectations or ways of working. The initiative about changing a representative might actually come from an experienced publisher who recognizes the signs that a relationship is not all that it could be.

Often, a key part of a negotiation is ensuring that a good working relationship persists. This helps the other side 'save face'. The purpose of negotiation is not to humiliate the other side – this would be aggressive. For example, where a publisher's representative reluctantly allows substantial discounts that may put them in an awkward position with their sales director, then the subscriber may be able to give assurances about making recommendations about the product, something that helps the representative 'save face', so that they feel able to do similar deals in the future.

In an ideal situation the same representative and negotiator will manage successive renewals of the same product. However, people change jobs, they get promoted and information about past negotiations gets lost. A subscriber is often impressed by a new representative who has 'done their homework', either via a handover meeting with the previous representative or by visiting the subscriber when accounts change hands. For the subscriber and publisher alike, keeping a record of previous dealings will be invaluable when the negotiator leaves the organization. That way their insights into the relationship can be preserved.

Subscribers will find it useful to record the following information about the publisher:

- the name and contact details of the representative
- who that representative reports to if they need their authorization to close a deal
- when negotiations were held in the past
- a brief summary of the results of the most recent negotiation, with any hints about future directions in prices
- any promises made by the publisher (e.g. about including new content at no extra charge)
- any promises made by the subscriber (e.g. providing feedback about a new interface)
- any user groups that exist.

Although a well established relationship is conducive to achieving a mutually acceptable outcome, both parties must be wary about becoming too close. It is not unusual for representatives and subscribers to become personal friends, but when this happens it becomes almost impossible for either side to feel comfortable in pushing for the best deal. That does not mean the subscriber refusing an invitation to a party hosted for clients or a drinks evening, but it does mean thinking carefully about attending events where the representative is including non-business friends. Nor does it mean not being interested in the lives of each other and exchanging information about experiences outside work. However, being hard-nosed in a deal when the previous weekend you were chatting with the representative and their friends at a parent–toddler group can be quite tough, if not impossible.

Being assertive

Many an information professional will have been on a course about how to be assertive. It is a key skill when dealing with the demands placed on them on a day-to-day basis. The nature of a representative means that they too are likely to have these skills. Assertiveness comes more naturally to some and also is easier is certain circumstances. Where money is involved, some people find being assertive more difficult. Chapter 1 on 'Preparation' is intended to give negotiators the confidence to be assertive in the final stages of the negotiation. If one side of the negotiation process is aggressive and another is passive, there will be at least one loser, if not both. If both are passive, then they are unlikely to have communicated their desires and both will walk away feeling dissatisfied. If both are aggressive, then the negotiation is highly likely to collapse and neither side will be willing to give any ground. If both sides are assertive, however, this will involve stating their case, knowing where to give ground, and ultimately both walking away from the close of the deal happy. In the simplest of negotiations, where there are just two sides, this can be demonstrated in a matrix form. Figure 3.2 shows how both sides being assertive is the ideal situation.

Aggressive			Passive
Win	I'm OK	I'm not OK	Lose
Lose	You're not OK	You're OK	Win
Lose	I'm not OK	I'm OK	Win
Lose	You're not OK	You're OK	Win
Insecure			Assertive

Figure 3.2   Negotiation matrix[4]

Negotiating the price

As mentioned in Chapter 1, it is far easier to formulate a stance if the quote has been obtained from the publisher ahead of the final negotiation. Unfortunately, it is rarely as simple as this since prices can go up, down or stay the same. Sometimes a transition to a new subscription model is needed (e.g. from named users to a site licence), making price comparisons difficult. In rare circumstances, the price may not be an area that the subscriber has an absolute need to negotiate upon.

Even if the price quoted is one that the subscriber can afford, they need to judge the sustainability of the pricing structure. For example, is a 10% price rise sustainable over a number of years when interest rates are far lower? If a subscriber accepts a price increase one year, without any query or undertakings from the publisher to make efforts to reduce the increase in future years, it might make it difficult to negotiate in future years as that rise was once seen as acceptable. There may be reasons why the subscriber accepts the larger than expected price increase, for example due to a very significant increase in content that is relevant to the organization. In these circumstances the subscriber might accept the price increase but explain that on this occasion their acceptance is for a particular reason and is not something that will occur under just any circumstances.

Is a large price increase justifiable?

It is also essential for the purchaser to be considerate about the publisher's situation. Where a quote is a good one and the publishing company might be a start-up, squeezing prices even further might jeopardize the existence of the product, which would mean that both parties would lose. Also consider past negotiations and where the subscribing organization has squeezed hard in the past – this might therefore be the year where it is necessary to be more understanding. If an organization gets a reputation for squeezing and squeezing every year no matter how good an offer, the good offers will cease to come through from the publisher.

As John Ruskin (1819–1900), author and philosopher, states:

It is unwise to pay too much but it is worse to pay too little. When you pay too much, you lose money – that is all. When you pay too little, you sometimes lose everything because what you bought was incapable of doing what it was bought to do. The common law of business balance prohibits paying a little and getting a lot – it can't be done. If you deal with the lowest bidder, it is well to add something for the risk you run, and if you do that, you will have enough to pay for something better.[5]

The language of negotiation

Certain phrases, which can be varied according to the format of the discussion (whether it be e-mail, a letter or a meeting), can be used to move the discussion along. The first item in the list below is an easy and flexible one to remember and is therefore ideal for a meeting scenario.

- The most useful two words are 'If . . . then . . .', which allow both parties to explore options and state their position without committing themselves. However, this option should not be used as a threat. It is more productive when used to explore options. For example:
  - If you are not prepared to come down on the price, *then* are you able to offer our other sites access at no extra cost?
  - If we were to reduce the asking price, *then* would you be prepared to subscribe for two years?
- How about . . .?
- Let's start at . . .?
- We understand your position. However . . .
- What do you want?
- Instead of 'But' use: 'Yes . . . and . . .', which is far more positive. When a sentence starts with 'Yes' people are more likely to listen compared to a sentence starting with 'But'. For example:
  - Yes, you would experience a higher price increase under that proposal, and with that increase you get access to more information.
- There is very little separating us.
- We have the same goal.

- We have both agreed that . . .
- I do not feel as though my requirements are being given due consideration.
- We have not made any movement. Where is it possible for you to compromise?

How do I get across my point?

You will need to be aware of when certain types of language are necessary. For example, exploratory questions such as the 'If . . . then . . .' and the 'How about' are good openers. Avoid too much use of 'you' where the negotiation is stalling, and instead use 'I'. In this way the negotiation does not fall into the trap of a 'blame game' where you say things like 'you are not listening'. Instead say 'I feel that I am not being listened to'. Where the negotiation seems to be going around in circles or the situation is unclear, a simple 'What do you want?' can be very effective, but typed into an e-mail without any other wording it will sound angry.

The sort of language that should be avoided includes:

- 'I hear you' – this is an overused phrase that has simply become annoying and usually indicates that the person is not really listening.
- 'But' – avoid starting a sentence with 'but' as people tend to switch off to negative-sounding sentences and will fail to hear the rest of the message.
- 'Take it or leave it' – this is not negotiating language: it is not giving a true choice.
- 'Trust me' – if you are having to say this it means that there is not a genuine trust between the negotiating parties and the problem needs to be addressed.

If no progress is being made, think about the types of question you are asking. For example, closed questions will not draw out the other person's true desires. Use open questions instead. Examples of open and closed questions are shown in Figure 3.3.

Closed questions	Open questions
Is this agreeable to you?	In what ways do you find this proposal agreeable?
Are you open to other suggestions?	I propose to make some suggestions. To what extent are you able to take these on board?
Are you able to amend the contract?	If I want amendments made to the contract, how does this happen?

Figure 3.3   Closed and open questions

Using objective criteria is a good way of securing information from the other side and thereby ultimately achieving your own goal. Objective criteria mean that information needs to be based on facts, and the principle of being seen to be fair is key. For example:

Sales rep:	The price is £6000.
Subscriber:	How do you get to that figure?
Sales rep:	That is our list price.
Subscriber:	Do you charge the same for every organization regardless of size?
Sales rep:	No, but that is what we would charge you.
Subscriber:	How do you view us?
Sales rep:	As a firm with 300 users.
Subscriber:	That figure is for all three of our offices. We only want this office to subscribe and it has 100 employees, many of whom do not use the product. We estimate that there would be about 30 users. Does that mean the price is now £600?
Sales rep:	We count potential users in the figure, and there are discounts for larger organizations. The lowest price is £1000 for a single user.
Subscriber:	I would think a fair price would be closer to £1000 than £6000 as we only have 30 users, not 300 users.

It is important to put the reason first and not the solution or demands. For example, if someone said to you 'It is imperative that you restrict the number of pages of our product that you view and reduce the number of users to a more reasonable level because . . .', then they will already be thinking of ways to counteract your demands — their attention will not be on the reasons. So always put the reason first and then the solution.

When a negotiation is stalling, then the frustration needs to be verbalized into phrases that express the feeling that nothing is being achieved or that the negotiators are not being listened to. In such situations it is necessary to become the driving force behind the negotiation and probe out any chinks of likely movement, and, if necessary, become quite blatant about how things have reached a standstill because of the inflexibility of the other party. However, be careful of accusing someone of inflexibility — it may also be affecting you!

When most points have been agreed but a few sticking points remain, it is essential to remain positive and not forget what has been achieved. Phrases such as 'There is very little separating us' or 'we have the same goal' can be useful. The phrase 'We have both agreed that . . .' is essential at the end of a negotiation as summing up has the dual advantage of avoiding any misunderstandings and keeping a record of what has been agreed for future reference.

In the rare situation where the purchaser and the publisher do not speak the same language, consider either a substitute who does speak the same language and who has been briefed about the goals, or an interpreter. The former means the negotiation is more likely to proceed smoothly but with reference back to the usual negotiator for authorization or clarification; the latter means that communication is likely to be stilted but has the authority and knowledge of the usual negotiator.

There are many arguments that the purchaser can make in favour of prices going down or remaining the same. Some of these are listed below:

Prices can remain static, going down in terms of inflation:

- where a publisher recognizes a good customer
- where there are competitor products
- when the size of the organization or user base has reduced
- where past years have seen consistent price increases
- where content has been removed from the database
- when the database has performed poorly
- if the model can be compared to that of a hard-copy subscription, where there is often a large up-front cost but in successive years the subscriber pays only for new content
- if changes to contract terms reduce the value of the product to the organization (e.g. material can no longer be disseminated)
- when the organization is a charity.

Arguments for accepting or justifying anything other than a modest increase include:

- when the content that has been asked for in the past has been added
- when the previous negotiations have been on the understanding that this year would see a larger increase
- when there is a substantial increase in the user base
- where the increase offers something else that is of value to the subscriber, such as the integration of content into other systems, the dissemination of information to third parties, or access to other locations.

Arguments for reducing a proposed large increase in price include:

- when successive large increases are not sustainable compared to the price paid in previous years
- when promises made at previous negotiations are compared to what was delivered (e.g. if they promised new content or better service)
- when price rises are completely unexpected and not budgeted for

Continued on next page

- when there are general budgetary constraints
- when the size of the organization has reduced
- when the price increase is justified on basis of new content
  — what value (if any) does that content have for the organization?
  — is there an option to exclude that content?
  — products are expected to improve over time and not remain static
- when the subscriber considers an alternative pricing model to keep the price manageable (e.g. ceasing a site licence and moving to a limited number of named users), which would result in a drastic reduction in revenues for the publisher
- when the price increase is not justified in any way (i.e. no new content, service or facility)
- if changes to contract terms reduce the value of the product

Dealing with emotions

Emotions very easily creep into a negotiation. Feelings range from anger and frustration to surprise and pleasure. It is important to be aware of how a particular proposal or stage of the negotiation is making you feel so that it does not take over the proceedings. Strong emotions will over-ride logic and assertiveness, both of which are needed in abundance in a good negotiation. Where an emotion is very strong it is going to be impossible to completely ignore it, but verbalizing it will help the negotiation along and let the other side know your true feelings and give them a better chance to act in a positive way to counteract the strength of feeling. Conversely, it is important to be aware of other people's feelings and give them the opportunity to manage their feelings or express them. Emotions are better managed in a non-face-to-face environment as there is the opportunity to escape from the situation that has created the emotion; in meetings this is not the case. If emotions start to cloud an issue in a meeting, then taking some 'time out' or re-convening the meeting at a later date is a good idea.

E-mail communications

E-mail is an excellent way to communicate because it allows you to keep track of the whole communication. Compared to face-to-face meetings, with e-mail there is not the same need to have done quite so much preparation. The MFP and WAP do not have to be hidden inside your head or written down on a folded piece of paper. However, it is not a perfect method, as without careful wording and management of the e-mails, misunderstandings can easily develop. E-mail etiquette is essential to prevent misunderstandings and misdirection. Hopefully, most individuals exercise good e-mail etiquette on a daily basis, but as so much hinges on negotiation, looking again at what is best practice is worthwhile.

The key rules for good e-mail etiquette include:

- *Read the e-mail properly before you reply to it* – many people get used to skim reading e-mails, but in a negotiation it is essential to keep your credibility and misreading something can lead to embarrassment and assertiveness tends to disappear. Misreading can also lead to incomplete replies and inaccurate information, taking the negotiation in completely the wrong direction.
- *A prompt response* – reply promptly, even if it is to say that due to other commitments you will not be able to give a full reply today. Ideally, give a date by when you expect to be able to reply.
- *Addressing the e-mail* – the salutation should be appropriate. In most negotiations the representative or publisher's first name are known to you and a simple 'Dear Clare' is perfectly fine.
- *Think about to whom to send the e-mail* – be cautious when using the 'reply to all' function – does everyone really need to be included? Be careful about copying in someone's boss if you feel that you are not getting anywhere with the representative as this can really annoy and embarrass them rather than helping you get what you want.
- *Use the subject line effectively* – this will help the message stand out in the recipient's inbox and also help you when it comes to filing and finding past e-mails.
- *Avoid using 'important', 'private' or 'urgent' tags* – some e-mail systems have the ability to mark e-mails as important, private or urgent. Where something is marked as private this means that the e-mail cannot be seen by anyone other than the named recipient. As a result, where a busy representative or head of information department has

their e-mail checked by an assistant, that e-mail will be missed. The over-use of the important or urgent tags also means that these tags cease to be useful, as the recipient no longer knows what is really important because all e-mails from that individual are marked as important or urgent.

- *Be concise but not curt* – overly wordy e-mails detract from the main message but overly brief e-mails with formal sign-offs can appear curt. For example, 'Will do, Regards, Cilla' in reply to an e-mail may be interpreted as cold and the recipient may think they have offended the sender in some way.
- *Answer all questions* – there is nothing more annoying or embarrassing than if someone has to follow up part of an e-mail. If you are only initially able to answer one part, make it clear which questions you intend to respond to later and give an idea of time scales.
- *Do not attach unnecessary files or forward or reply unnecessarily* – it does not look very professional to reply to an e-mail from the previous year's negotiations, even if it does contain a lot of useful information. This implies that the sender has not bothered to store the contact details in their address book and the additional content also detracts from the new negotiations in hand. If one of the negotiators is new and needs information that they cannot get from their end, then they should ask for it and it can be more appropriately sent as an attachment to an e-mail. On the other hand, it is useful to have all the information of a current issue all in one e-mail, so using the reply function and including the previous threads can save time and prevent misunderstandings.
- *If attaching files, consider the format* – be cautious about attaching files that are not in standard formats such as .doc, .pdf or .tif as the recipient may not have the software to read the file. Do not attach a document that is password protected.
- *Do not spell out an entire word in CAPITALS* – the use of capitals in an e-mail implies 'shouting' and can therefore be seen as very rude.
- *Use proper grammar, punctuation and spelling* – this avoids any misunderstanding or embarrassment on the part of either sender or receiver. Avoid 'texting' language, which is more and more infiltrating

the world of e-mail. For example, spell out fully 'Please would you send us a quotation for the renewal of our subscription to product x' rather than 'Pse wd u . . .'. The overuse of punctuation (!!!) can be seen as amusing by some, but should not be used in a business-to-business environment.

- *Structure your e-mail* – do not put all the text in one block as this makes it difficult to digest. A few small short paragraphs, bullet points or two or three brief sentences usually work best.
- *Signing off* – include your name and the organization's standard signature, which usually contains an address and telephone contact details. If in doubt, check that the contact details are included. Sometimes there is 'hidden' information in the e-mail footer that only those outside the organization will get to see, such as a disclaimer.
- *Out of office* – if you have this function, use it. Make it clear when you are due to return and to whom to direct urgent queries in your absence.

One major problem with e-mail is that there is no guarantee that the recipient has received it, unlike a telephone conversation or meeting where you know that they have got the message. While there are tools such as read-receipt, this does not always work, especially between different e-mail platforms. In the absence of a response, and when an e-mail is really important, it is a good idea to follow up between an hour and a day later with a telephone call. For ease of communication it is essential to maintain continuity of contact wherever possible, so the same person should deal with all the e-mails regarding the renewal of a single product. It can create confusion if a different person responds to an e-mail because the new recipient may not be aware what level of knowledge the sender has about the entire exchange and will wonder who to reply to – the new sender, the original sender or both.

As mentioned earlier in this chapter, rarely is negotiation formed of one method of communication, but if the bulk of the communication is by e-mail, then examples of how this might take place, and the sort of wording used, are outlined below.

Preparation: refer back to the previous year's agreement

Before communications commence it is essential to refer to the previous year's correspondence or the location where information about the previous year's negotiation is summarized. This applies to both publisher and purchaser. Start with the quote from last year and what was agreed and check whether any caveats were made at that negotiation. For example, it may have been agreed that if the product was renewed on a like-for-like basis, then the increase in price would be no more than 3%.

First e-mail

Each organization will have their own timeline based on budget submissions, scheduling of other meetings and particular times of the year which are busy. A sample timeline is given in Appendix 2. If the organization has not received an e-mail from their representative about the renewal at least a month before the deal needs to come to a conclusion, then the organization should be the one to start the process. When there is an established relationship between publisher and purchaser, the publisher should be fully aware of the purchaser's timelines and will most likely be the one to get in touch first. When the publisher contacts the purchaser their opening salvo is usually something along the lines of 'it's that time of year again. . . . is it convenient for you to discuss the renewal of product X?' At the other end of the spectrum, the publisher may go in rather abruptly with a figure that they have in mind.

When the purchaser initiates the communications it is useful for the publisher to understand what the deadlines are from the outset, so this information should be included in the e-mail. It can be very frustrating for someone used to almost instantaneous responses to their e-mails to wait for several days, but this may be normal for the person at the other end and they are unaware that they are creating a bad impression. If a reply is needed by a particular time to get things moving along, then this must be clearly explained. Language such as 'at your earliest convenience' is not very clear at all and also sounds very stuffy.

Following up

Once a quote is on the electronic table it will be one of three things to the subscribing organization: a pleasant surprise, a nasty surprise, or just about what you were expecting. Although a nasty surprise will require more time to compose a response, even a pleasant surprise should not be responded to with a simple 'OK'.

When a quote is a pleasant surprise and the organization is content with the contract terms, a simple acceptance and confirmation that all terms you currently enjoy remain the same will bring the 'negotiation' to a swift and easy end. In truth, a negotiation has not really taken place as neither party has had to make any movement or concessions. The negotiator needs to make a judgement about whether it is worth their time to pursue the matter further or accept the terms. The advantage of e-mail (in this instance, to the purchaser) is that the publisher will not have seen the broad smile that emerged on the negotiator's face when they read the message.

Even when there is a pleasant surprise this does not mean that there is no room for movement. There may be some element of the Most Favoured Position that would merit being explored in more detail, or consideration of the long-term cost of the product. For example, if the increase in price is a nominal 1%, the subscribing organization could enquire about increases in future years, wording the e-mail in an assumptive tone, indicating that they anticipate that the small price rise is a trend that the publisher intends to continue, without committing to additional years. It may be that the publisher does not have a long-term plan and is unable to commit to any undertakings, but at least the subscriber has made the point that acceptance of a small price rise does not mean that this can be offset by a large price rise in subsequent years, putting the negotiator in a good position for the future. Planning a budget can be very difficult if a publisher has small or no increases for several years and then a massive price hike.

The negotiator can also take the initiative when there is a pleasant surprise and pursue an even better deal. If they feel it is in the organization's best interests, they may suggest to the publisher that they renew for two years at zero price increase, guaranteeing revenue stream for the publisher.

If the quote is just about what you were expecting, visit the MFP again and consider how much room for movement there is. The subscribing negotiator can use language that creates a sense of movement or progression, such as 'Although this nearly meets what we are looking for, we were hoping for an increase that would more fully reflect interest rates at the present time'. This is not saying how much the subscriber is willing to pay, what is in their budget, or making any sort of commitment. As mentioned previously, if past negotiations for the same product were pursued vigorously, this may be a year to accept the proposed sum. Negotiation is about gaining the right balance between what you want and what you can accept.

If a negotiator relishes receiving an e-mail that proposes a huge increase in subscription price with no explanation or added benefit, then they are either being too aggressive or there has been a breakdown in the relationship between customer and client. Sentiments will hopefully be more of disappointment at seeing such a high price and recognition that this proposal needs to be considered with reference to material gathered in the preparation process. In these situations an e-mail to the effect that 'the figure quoted is vastly outside the range we were expecting to pay so we will have to spend some time looking into this' will buy the purchaser some time.

A major advantage of e-mail is that it is possible to discuss a proposal with colleagues and ask opinions of users without the sender of the original e-mail necessarily knowing. Often something originally considered essential may not be seen as so important once the user is aware of how much the product actually costs. Some organizations have policies about discussing prices with any person other than a core team of negotiators, but as a general rule sharing pricing information internally is a good way of provoking a valuable reply. Avoid just forwarding an e-mail with the query 'what do you think?' unless the person is expecting it and knows what they are to comment on. Such a statement should include:

- the product in question
- the stage of the negotiation
- the proposed price compared to the previous year, preferably as both sums and as percentages

- the background facts, which should be kept to a minimum but included if considered useful, such as the number of users.

An example of such an e-mail is shown in Figure 3.4.

Date: 14 March 06
To: john.colleague@organization.com
From: negotiator@organization.com

Dear John,
The proposal below from our representative at Publisher X quotes a renewal price for Product Y of £10,000. Last year we paid £8000 for the same level of access. This represents an increase of 25%.

The product is due for renewal at the end of next month and as one of ten users of this product I would welcome your opinion as to the value of the product with regard to the work that you do.

Any feedback you might be able to supply on the product will help us in our negotiations. I am hoping to respond to their proposal in the next two days.

Best regards

A Negotiator
Library & Information Centre

Date: 13 Mar 06
To: negotiator@organization.com
From: rep@publisher.co.uk

Dear Subscriber,

Further to your e-mail enquiring about renewal prices I am pleased to advise you that we can offer you a renewal price of £10,000 which is a substantial saving on our list price of £13,500 for up to ten subscribers.

Should you wish to discuss this please do not hesitate to give me a call

Kind regards

A Rep
Publisher X

Figure 3.4　Evaluating a proposal with colleagues

Consideration also needs to be given as to whether the original e-mail from the publisher needs to be included at all. In the above example the end-user who is being asked for their opinion may just see that there is a £3500 saving on the list price and think this is a bargain without considering that £8000 to £10,000 is a 25% increase. There is also the additional danger with e-mail that the end-user will contact the publisher direct rather than mediate through the contact within the subscribing organization. Asking the end-user how valuable the product is to their work (or studies) will assist the negotiator in devising their WAP.

This middle stage may take a few e-mails before both parties feel they are close to a conclusion. Where a stalemate persists, then it is usually necessary to change the method of communication to either the telephone or a meeting.

Determining whether it is the best deal and concluding that deal

Knowing when the offer on the table is one that cannot be pushed any further is something that can to some extent come from reading the tone and wording of the e-mail. Has the publisher indicated that they have used their last option to obtain a good discount or get the best terms? For example, they might have had to refer to their superior to confirm that the discount being sought is permitted. Other indications are that the other party has conceded some ground over the course of a number of e-mails.

In summary, you will know when you have secured the best available deal when:

- several e-mails have been exchanged and movement has been made
- comparisons have been made with what has been paid in the past
- comparisons have been made with what has been paid by other organizations – some publish these as part of a consortium arrangement
- suggestions to the other party about new terms or better prices are not being well received
- reference has already been made to a higher authority to get permission for that price.

When the subscriber finally gets a proposal that they will accept, this is also the opportunity to sum up. Summing up is important as it ensures that there are no misunderstandings. It also puts the person who does the summing up in an assertive position. Wording such as 'we agree to pay £8,750 in monthly instalments in a like-for-like renewal of Product Y' is sufficient but a bit brief. It can be dressed up with a sentence or two providing feedback about the product, or saying how happy the organization is that negotiations have come to a fruitful conclusion.

✓ To summarize using e-mail for communication:

- Refer back to the previous year's communications to get the background.
- Start by either responding to a proposal or asking for a proposal to be sent.
- If a delay is likely, respond to the effect that time to consider will mean a brief delay.
- Maintain good e-mail etiquette at all times.
- Who needs to be consulted within the organization or within the publishing house?
- Depending on whether the proposal is close to the MFP, consider how necessary it is to pursue a better deal.
- Make a counter-proposal if necessary.
- Judge when there is no further ground to be gained by the use of language, responsiveness to suggestions and the use of higher authorities.
- Sum up what has been agreed.

Meetings

For large, important deals, a meeting is usually the normal course of action. Meetings are also useful where other methods of communication have reached a stalemate and neither party has reached a satisfactory position. The advantages of meetings are that they are face to face, there are less likely to be misunderstandings as body language can be read, and they build up the relationship between publisher and purchaser. Meetings are also compact – there is no need to wait several days for a reply to a query or suggestion. It is often assumed that a meeting requires the parties to come to a conclusion there and then, but this is not the case. While in an ideal situation both subscriber and publisher will come away from a single meeting with an agreement, no side should feel pressured into achieving this in one sitting.

This section assumes a face-to-face meeting but most of the advice can also be applied to video-conferencing situations. The key difference with the latter format is that those involved in the meeting need to understand how the technology works so that it does not make them feel uncomfortable.

Scheduling a meeting

A meeting should be scheduled at the convenience of the subscriber. Thought should be given to deadlines (when it is necessary to come to a conclusion), the availability of staff, any preparation work that needs to be done and the location of the meeting. If the subscriber has to travel to a main city to meet representatives and fit a number of negotiations into just a few days (to cut down on travel and hotel costs), then this also needs to be borne in mind. The same goes for the publisher, who is the one more likely to be doing the travelling. Meetings can be scheduled either by telephone or by e-mail. The key negotiator is then responsible for ensuring that the appointment is in the diaries of those who need to attend.

In Chapter 1 we discussed understanding your own organization and its processes. The same applies to meetings that are held in one of the other party's own premises. For example, there may be a requirement to notify security so that they can issue visitor badges, or internal budget codes may need to be assigned for the cost of any refreshments, and a meeting room may need to be booked. Even if the negotiator of the meeting has the luxury of someone else to organize the room booking for them, they will still need to pass on a certain amount of information:

- who needs to be involved with the organization
- how long the meeting should be
- who needs to be invited from the other side and what are their contact details

- whether there is a time period during which they can search for mutually available dates and times
- subject of the meeting
- whether there needs to be any information, such as an agenda or background information, in the body of the invitation if using an electronic calendar
- if any special equipment is needed, such as a flipchart
- whether a preparation meeting is also required.

The amount of time to allow for the meeting does not necessarily mean that the meeting will actually take that long. The meeting slot should not be longer than an hour where there are just two parties involved. Where there is a complicated multi-party meeting, which may involve numerous delegates, break-out sessions and re-convening, then it is not unreasonable to expect this to take the best part of a day.

Awareness of the number of people likely to attend from the other party is also essential to prevent any side feeling intimidated or becoming either passive or aggressive rather than assertive. Once acceptances for the meeting have been received, then a confirmation of the meeting date and who will be attending is useful to the other party. If a meeting is scheduled in good time, then it is not such a dire situation if it has to be postponed because of other commitments, fire drills (it does happen – honest!) or illness.

The agenda of the meeting should also be made clear. Ideally, there will be just one item on the agenda, that of negotiation. It is not advisable to combine meetings about different subjects when one of them is negotiation. For example, if a representative were to make a presentation on planned upgrades to the product and then have discussions about the price and terms, the subscriber is put in a difficult position as they have just heard all about the wonderful developments that are due to take place with regard to the product.

If the meeting is a substantial one which is likely to take most of a day, then the agenda should be more detailed so that the negotiators have the necessary paperwork and background information to hand. A sample agenda might include:

- *contract terms* – discuss the format of the contract (whether it is to be a standard one), the publisher's contract and any points which either side are not happy with
- *extent of contract* – the number of people or locations where the licence operates
- *wish list* – a list of items that are not essential but are desirable, such as access to an archive should the subscription cease
- *the price.*

When a meeting straddles the lunch period, it should also be made clear to visitors what the lunch arrangements are, such as sandwich provision in the room or something more substantial in a nearby restaurant.

Where to hold a meeting

It is important for the subscribing organization to feel comfortable about where the meeting is held. If there are suitable rooms, then holding a meeting at the subscriber's premises is the most ideal situation. Holding a meeting at the subscriber's premises means they will be calmer, more confident in their own surroundings as well as saving time and travelling costs. It is not advisable to hold the meeting over a business meal or drink as there will be distractions, ranging from ordering food to other diners. Social events also usually entail one party potentially feeling under an obligation to the paying party. While social events such as an annual party given by the publisher are a fine way of maintaining a good publisher–subscriber relationship, they are best not mixed with the topic of negotiation. When suitable rooms are not available at the subscriber's premises other options present themselves, ranging from the publisher's premises to a small meeting room at a hotel that caters for business meetings. The latter option may be required when either the publisher or the subscriber has to travel some distance in order to attend the meeting.

Where there is a large multi-party deal or consortium arrangement that is in the early stages and is likely to take some time, one meeting room may not be sufficient. To ensure that negotiators do not feel 'trapped' it is a good idea to have a 'break-out' room where one side can go and discuss proposals and tactics as they go along.

A meeting about a meeting

When more than one person within an organization is attending the meeting, it is worth spending at least ten minutes discussing how the meeting is going to be handled and who is responsible for what areas. This should not be held more than a week before the actual meeting otherwise too much time will have passed and the tactics will be forgotten. If more than one participant from the same organization is going to be present, then decide who is going to be the main spokesperson. This avoids any chance of the meeting descending into confusion because too many people want to put their point across, not necessarily in an orderly manner. This also means that if there are, for example, two people from the subscribing organization and just one from the publisher, the publisher is clearer about to whom to direct their conversation and they do not feel outnumbered by too many people talking in succession.

The preparation meeting will clarify what are the MFP, the WAP and whether there is a BATNA. If there is more than one person involved in the negotiation, it can be useful to have an informal 'nice guy' and 'bad guy'. This ensures that if the meeting is going in one direction only, for example turning into a blame scenario, then the 'good guy' can bring in a comment about how well the product is received by end-users, stopping the negative flow. In comparison, if the meeting is circling around the point and not getting to the main concerns, then the 'bad guy' can contribute with something to shake the meeting up; this might range from reliability problems to re-verbalizing in a more abrupt manner the key points up for negotiation.

The layout of the meeting room

Wherever possible the meeting room should be an appropriate size for the number of people attending. An enormous, wide, boardroom table that seats 20 is not ideal when there are just two people in the room. If there is no choice, then the solution is to sit around one corner of the table rather than across a large expanse of table. Conversely, where there is a meeting involving 20 people to discuss, for example, the wish-list for a consortium agreement, then the room must not be too cramped and thought needs to be given to the format of the meeting. For example, is it a presentation by the key negotiator to interested participants that will need a 'theatre-style' layout, or is it an inclusive meeting where everyone needs the chance to contribute, in which case a round or boardroom table setting is more appropriate? Unless in a theatre-style setting, no table at all makes the scene too informal. Avoid the sofa-style setting. Unless the character of the visitor is known very well, a very informal setting should be used with caution. Check with the other party whether they need any equipment. For example, in convoluted negotiations it is useful to have a flipchart to write down what has been agreed.

The main considerations for the host are:

- Use a room that is an appropriate size for the number attending the meeting.
- Think about the layout of the room:
  - Avoid an intimidatory layout such as a large expanse of table
  - Use an overly informal setting such as a sofa style arrangement with caution
  - Ensure that no one is put in a position where they have to squint owing to beaming sunlight – they might think they are deliberately being put off.
- Ensure that there are refreshments, even if it is just water.
- If there is a phone in the room, make sure it is diverted.
- Ensure there are no remnants of a previous meeting, such as flipchart pages or handouts, lying around.
- Coats and bags of visitors should be stowed away or hung up so as not to make the visitors uncomfortable by having them slung across the back of a chair.
- Make sure that any equipment, such as a flipchart, pens or paper, is available.

The structure of the meeting

- Introductions
- Test assumptions
  - Go over what information is already available, such as a proposal supplied via e-mail or information about new modules (e.g.

'I assume that the new module is included in the renewal quote').
* Explore and exchange information
    - Explain the main reasons for having problems with the proposal (e.g. budgetary pressures or a successful trial of a competitor product).
* Make suggestions
    - To get the negotiation going use the 'if . . . then . . .' language and invite a response.
* Listen
    - Listen to the response and, if necessary, allow a moment or two of silence rather than jumping in with another question.
* Respond
    - Use positive language wherever possible.
* Make counter-proposals
    - Go through the previous three stages again and again until a solution is reached, building upon the previous responses.
* Reach agreement
    - Once all issues have been resolved summarize what has been agreed and what the next steps are, such as to expect a newly drafted terms and conditions.
    - If there are any issues outstanding, agree what these are and how they will be resolved, via either another meeting or clarification by e-mail or a telephone call.

Introductions

Introductions are an important part of any meeting. What needs to be conveyed are brief facts about who you are, your role, and to what degree you are negotiating. For example:

I am Joe Brown. I am the Library and Information Centre Manager here in our London office, with a specific responsibility for online resources. I do not have the authority to make decisions for the national network, only for this office. However, I do have the authority to make a decision today provided it falls within our budgetary constraints.

If this is not the first time that the parties have met, then these formalities do not need to be carried out. New publisher representatives are often interested in how the organization is structured, who makes the decision about what products to buy and the remit of the person with whom they are liaising.

The visitors also need to be made comfortable by the offering of refreshments and taking of their coats. If necessary, explain the location of toilets and other facilities.

A major difference between a negotiation meeting and many other meetings is that there is no obvious chairperson. However, this role may be needed to ensure that the meeting progresses and does not go too far off track. Each side must be prepared to take on the role at moments they see fit.

Test assumptions

The dialogue should commence with clarification of why the parties are meeting, for example stating that the discussions are for a like-for-like renewal for product X. This also sends a message to the other negotiator that the intention is to keep the meeting very focused. The next move is to share what information is being used as a starting point, such as the current price and terms plus a proposal that has been supplied for the forthcoming year. The next stage is to make some assumptions which are a very quick and easy way of getting a point across. For example:

> I assume that there will be no surprises as the product has remained much the same and we are not looking for a change in the contract terms.

The reaction of the other party will quickly indicate how far apart the two parties are from their MFP. Questions also avoid the build-up of aggression and give the other side the opportunity to respond in a positive rather than a defensive way. For example:

> Do I understand that we have been paying substantially more than the list price?

rather than:

> We've been paying more than the list price for the past year
> or more.

Make suggestions

Either party can become blinkered and stuck on a straight path that offers little in the way of flexibility. One way out of this is to be inventive with regard to the suggestions that are made. For example:

> Your suggestion of a price rise to £8000 from £7000
> represents more than a 10% increase. We propose that if you
> must have this sort of price rise, then it needs to be spread
> over at least three years to better reflect interest rates as they
> stand now. Would you consider a three-year deal where in
> the forthcoming year we pay closer to what we are currently
> paying, gradually escalating to the figure you propose?

When making a suggestion, it is an ideal time to use the 'If . . . then . . .' language. Other possibilities and examples are included below:

- '*If* you can come down on the price, *then* we may be able to look at a longer-term subscription.'
- '*If* we issued a press release saying we were subscribing to your product, *then* would you be able to accommodate a price freeze?'
- '*If* the price is not flexible, *then* are the locations where we can use the product more flexible?'
- '*If* you agree to this price this year, *then* we will agree a price cap should you want to renew next year.'

Coming up with ideas or options

Coming up with some possible solutions relies on a number of things:

- *Preparation done earlier* – Ideally you will have done some research before the negotiation phase and this will prompt ideas. For example, a poor performance of the database over the previous year might prompt the idea that if the price cannot be negotiated downwards, then there will need to be a service-level agreement, an extension of the subscription term or a refund option.

- *Empathy* – The ability to empathize with the other side will enable a negotiator to see their point of view, which will help with ideas.
- *Understanding reasons why a situation may not be attractive to the other side* – If you can understand the reasons why a proposal may not be attractive, then there is a higher likelihood of being able to turn the reason around or make it appear more attractive. Analysis of the problem will highlight any particular sticking point, and it may be just one element that can be eliminated.
- *Being able to see what the consequences of a particular action would be* – This can 'sell' an idea to the other side if it can be demonstrated that there is an advantage in pursuing this idea.
- *Identifying mutually beneficial options* – There are many instances when there does not have to be 'give and take', but both sides can gain. For example, it may be attractive for a small publisher to get a subscription in full up front, and to achieve this they are willing to give a substantial discount over what the price would be if the subscriber were paying monthly.

Listen and take note

It is very hard in a meeting to be silent, but there are times when it is necessary. Once a suggestion has been made it is vital to wait and listen to the response. Asking another question will only create a wider gulf of unanswered questions. Where a response says that no answer is immediately available and the query has to be passed on to a higher authority or considered away from the meeting environment, then make a note of what is still outstanding. Depending on the size, likely duration and complexity of the meeting, nominate one person to be the official note taker.

Avoid language such as 'I hear you' or 'I hear where you're coming from'. These are rather stock phrases and usually serve to annoy rather than achieve anything useful.

Respond

It is important to answer every question, even if the answer is 'I don't know' or 'I will have to investigate that possibility further'. If the answer is complex, or several questions were asked at once, the question should be included in the answer. For example:

> Your key concern is to be able to disseminate the information to third parties in the course of your normal business. We don't have a problem with this provided that the information is not separately charged for and it isn't done on a regular basis for the same third party. We will get the terms of the contract amended to clarify this. We expect this will take a couple of days for our legal team to sort out.

If the response includes an action needed on your part, then make this clear. Without this information tying up all the agreed points becomes more difficult. It is also good to give a timescale for any actions. Giving these details ensures that there is no room for misunderstanding. The example given above states that in order for the information to be disseminated to third parties the contract will need to be amended, and also gives an approximation of how long that might take.

Counter-proposals

Refer back to what has been offered so that it is clear to the offering party that it has been fully understood, but then balance this with something more akin to what is actually being sought. For example, the publisher might counter the example given by the supplier above with:

> Your suggestion of a three-year deal with prices gradually rising from the current figure to £8000 over that three-year period is close to something that we can work with. The necessity at the moment is for the price to rise to reflect developments made to the interface, so I would suggest an initial rise in the first year to £8000 and there being no price rise the following two years.

Other language that can be used in the counter-proposal stage includes:

* 'Yes that is a good suggestion, and I would make it even better by . . .'
* 'I see your position; however, our situation is . . .'
* 'We can build upon that proposal by . . .'

Reach an agreement and conclude

At some stage in the meeting it will be apparent that further discussion is either not needed or that 'time out' is necessary. The latter might be for just a few minutes or for several weeks. Reconvening a meeting is not admitting failure: it is just allowing time for more information to be gathered, suggestions and proposals to be discussed, and for the meeting to be recommenced at a more advanced stage. Where a meeting is brought to a halt by one party, it needs to be made clear why. This gives the other side an opportunity to either agree or disagree with the decision. If another meeting is required or the outstanding points can be solved in another way, this also needs to be made clear.

In some situations only one of the negotiators has the authority to conclude a deal, but this has not been apparent until one party says that what has been discussed sounds goods, but they need to take it to someone else for approval. This puts the person who has to seek approval at an advantage as they can get back at a later time or date and say they need something more. In this situation the person who does have the authority is within their rights to renegotiate too.

Summing up at the end of a meeting is essential. When summarizing it is vital that negative points do not overshadow what has actually been achieved. Be positive about what has been achieved, but if the negotiations are not yet complete, be cautious about raising expectations too high. If no movement towards respective goals has been made, disappointment can be expressed so that the other party is in no doubt about the true feelings.

Language that can be used includes:

* We need to clarify . . .
* In my opinion we have got as far as we can for the moment . . .

- I think we have achieved a lot today
- To summarize what has been agreed . . .
- This has been a very positive meeting
- We are disappointed that this meeting . . . We will have to go away and review how best to go forward.

Body language

Body language is an entirely separate discipline so we will only cover the basics here. Being able to read body language as well as being conscious of the message that is being sent out by your own body language can only help progress a negotiation.

Body language can:

- give you an indication of how certain someone is about a statement they have made and give you an opportunity to probe deeper if necessary
- let you know how confident the other people are
- help you emphasize a point
- influence
- be intimidating if used aggressively
- demonstrate that you are seeking information
- demonstrate attention and interest.

Eye contact

Too much eye contact can unsettle or intimidate the other person, whereas the complete absence of eye contact can indicate 'shiftiness' or not paying attention. Withdrawal of eye contact by lowering the eyes is usually seen as an act of submission. Therefore it is necessary to maintain a good balance of eye contact in a negotiation scenario — not too much and not too little.

Facial expression

It is possible to support an interpretation of a proposal or suggestion by facial expression. Conversely, it is possible to reveal or read inner thoughts through facial movements where the verbal message may be very different.

Facial expression can also be used as a means of changing the direction of a negotiation (see Table 3.2).

Table 3.2   Facial expression in aiding negotiation

Situation	Facial expression
Bored and cannot get a word in edgeways	Look up and sigh
Don't believe them	Raise eyebrows, purse lips and tilt head
Want to encourage more of the same/agreement	Nod and smile
Confused	Frown and look to the side
Trying to get a point across/determination	Face forward, close eye contact
I'm listening	Smile, periodic eye contact, occasional nod
Disappointment	Slight shake of head, sag of shoulders, pursed lips, look down, small sigh or audible breath through nose
Firm disagreement	Firm shake of head, eye contact, audible breath through nose
It's only a suggestion	Raise eyebrows, gesture with hands opening outward, slight tilt of head
I'm thinking about it	Hands clasped, possibly in front of face; slight tilt of head, eyes looking away

Style statements

Impressions can be based on what you wear. The impression that needs to be created is one of professional confidence without appearing to be trying too hard or being too austere. Therefore, if someone is comfortable in a crisp suit, then that is fine; if they work in an industry that is well known for its casual wear, then that is also fine. Overly formal clothing might be intimidating for some, whereas overly casual clothes might give the wrong message, i..e. that the person is either not very professional or does not consider the meeting very important.

Accessories can also play a part. Too much jewellery, or electronic devices such as an MP3 player clipped on to a lapel, might distract the other negotiator and hinder eye contact. If the organization has a 'dress down' day, judge whether you should either advise the guests of this or amend your own dress code for the day so that they do not feel uncomfortable or out of place.

Business objective

It is useful if the negotiator's method of achieving their objective can be identified. This can then help the other negotiator react in an appropriate manner. American psychologist David McClelland identifies three types of business objective:[6]

- affiliation
- achievement
- power.

The aim of the *affiliator* is to create an atmosphere of good feelings and cohesion; they are assertive in a positive way and tend to bring out the best in people. Affiliators can often be distinguished by their keenness to greet people, their ability to chat about things other than the immediate agenda items and their use of smiles and eye contact. They often arrive ahead of time.

The aim of the *achiever* is to get the task done in the most efficient manner. They usually arrive on time rather than early or late, and will constantly force the agenda back on track. The achiever will use varied eye contact and will be keen to sit close to the decision-makers or to people they suspect might block their proposals or prevent a speedy outcome.

The aim of the *power seeker* is to be the one in control. In a negotiation this means they may be less flexible than others. They usually try to place themselves in a position that aids their objective, either at the head of the table or next to decision-makers. Power seekers may have a habit of speaking over people if they are not getting their own way, and over-using eye contact to intimidate others.

Body language summary

Body language can help assist in all the stages of the negotiation. For example, when giving someone the time to respond to a query, sit back and relax. Do not sit on the edge of the seat and drum fingers, appearing desperate for an immediate reply. Take the time to read the other person's body language, determine if it is necessary to reinvigorate the meeting by making bolder suggestions, or look at them and see whether the proposal is confusing them and needs rephrasing.

Internal negotiations

In many negotiations an information professional may have to negotiate with others within their organization, for example with their finance officer; a publisher's representative may also have to negotiate internally, for example with the person who sets their targets.

Making people feel involved

People like to be flattered. If a complicated negotiation gets to a critical point and only at the last minute is someone else consulted or asked for their input, this may make them feel like second best. If there is someone important to be consulted, be aware of their preferences. They may like to be consulted only on very rare occasions as they trust you and they are a busy person. Alternatively, they may like to be able to make some small input early on in the negotiation phase so that they feel included, and as a result will be more likely to help out more fully if the need arises at a later stage.

Justifying a subscription

When an information professional has to justify a vast expenditure on one product, it is often to an individual or board who have little understanding of the product or how it is used. All they see is a large sum of money against a name that means little to them. The sort of information they want is what difference that product makes to the organization. It may be necessary to provide either a verbal explanation or a document explaining why the expenditure is justified. The sort of information they want includes:

- by whom the product is used, especially key personnel
- for what purpose a product is used
- whether the organization can operate without doing the task that the product is used for
- whether there are any cheaper alternatives and why these are not used
- whether there is an alternative way of getting the information (e.g. manually compiling the information from hard copy) and, if so, how long does this take, or can this task be outsourced
- what are the consequences of ceasing a subscription, for example:
  - having to subscribe to previously cancelled hard-copy journals
  - paying for document delivery services, with estimated volumes, costs and mention of the consequences of the slower service
  - having to remove links from catalogues or intranets where, if there are many deep links, this could be a potentially huge task.

All the information needs to be hard facts presented in a clear, easily digestible format, and cannot be in put in vague terms. Note the use of precise numbers and figures in the re-worded example below. For example:

> Not having this single database means that the task will take much much longer and will require the use of a variety of non-authoritative internet sources.

should be re-worded to say:

> Users in Department Y need to find background information on a company and individuals before taking on a new client under a legal obligation to Regulatory Authority Z. The consequences of not subscribing, at a cost of £30,000 p.a., to product X will mean that:
>
> • users in Department Y will have to use at least seven separate non-authoritative sources on the free internet, and then collate that information in a meaningful way.

- each search and collation will take a minimum of 25 minutes compared to the present time of three minutes. At an average of ten searches per user per day, this equates to just over four hours a day compared to the existing 30 minutes a day. There are 20 users in Department Y so this equates to an extra 70 hours per day or ten extra members of staff at an estimated annual cost of £250,000.
- any advice based on that information will have a much higher likelihood of being out of date, inaccurate, or at times unavailable, potentially breaching the firm's obligations to the Regulatory Authority.

There are no alternative subscription-based products currently on the market that achieve the same or similar results.

Less important points that could be made should be left out. For example, users needing to attend a training session on how to access and use the alternatives is less important than the amount of time needed to do the alternative style of search. Too much information will cloud the points that will sway the decision-makers and should only be given if they actually ask for more information. Negative language should also be avoided. For example, language such as 'it will take too long' or 'it's not as nice' are not very helpful to those who do not know what they are comparing and just sound like 'whingeing'.

In order to build up trust internally it is also essential to be honest about a product and not to 'talk it up' or overly praise it if it is not essential. Praising every product and making them all sound essential will make the 'powers that be' look more suspiciously on the good points that are mentioned.

Areas for negotiation other than price

Contract terms (see Chapter 2) are closely allied to negotiation of aspects of a subscription other than price. It is rare to enter a negotiation just about the price, although it may be one of the key points. For example, it is often the case that a negotiation is about the number of users as well as the price. Where the parties are not willing to move on price, then other aspects of the subscription may become more important to justify that product's value to the subscribing organization or the cheaper price to the publisher. Outlined below are some issues which are worth negotiating on. These may or may not have a monetary value. Some of these arguments may add weight to a reduction in price and so become very interdependent on each other. These can be suggestions put forward by either publisher or subscriber.

Users

Depending on the pricing model, it may be possible to get the 'per capita' price down by getting extra users added to a subscription. This may then make it easier for the subscriber to justify to others internally the additional cost.

For example, the product used to cost £5000 and the new price of £6000 is non-negotiable. There are five users at present but the publisher responds to the suggestion 'If I am prepared to pay the proposed sum, then can you double our number of users?' with 'While I cannot double the number of users, I am prepared to give free access to two extra users'. This means that the previous £1000 per capita price has gone down to just over £850.

Access for other locations

A product may have specific relevance to one location but passing interest to other locations. For example, a database of art images is key to the History of Art faculty at a university, but of little interest to most other departments, which may be at different locations. Another example might be a database of English case law which will only have occasional interest outside England and Wales. Subscribers might argue that for consistency access at other locations would be ideal but not essential, and the publisher might agree to do this for little or no cost.

Another example to be considered is where organizations have users who regularly travel. Do the contract terms permit remote access and, if so, can this be for extended periods such as secondment? By giving wider access to non-key areas a publisher will gain a lot of goodwill for little or no outlay.

Training

Not all publishers offer free training, or when they do it may be only available to large accounts. Asking for free training may therefore be of benefit to the subscriber. Clarify whether it is in-house training or at the publisher's premises. This is quite important if the publisher is miles away from the subscriber, perhaps in another country. This argument is particularly useful for the sole practitioner, who may feel they have little weight in the negotiation process.

Extra modules

In a modular product there may be key modules that an organization is happy to pay for, but others that have little value but which may be dipped into occasionally. Some databases are structured in such a way that content that is not subscribed to comes up with error messages or other annoying features, such as prompting for a password when the rest of the database is accessed via IP authentication. Getting extra modules 'thrown in' for free or a nominal sum can avoid this latter problem. Being offered the modules at a 'bargain' price may just be a means for the publisher to get more revenue.

The subscriber needs to work out the benefit to the organization, whether any more technical work needs to be done and, if the price is based on usage levels, whether having more modules will be desirable or not.

Renewal guarantee/multi-year deal

If the subscriber is pushing for a price reduction, either they or the publisher might suggest that in return for the price reduction they will extend their commitment to two or more years. This extended term should be conjoined with a clear indication of what the price will be, otherwise an undertaking to renew is likely to penalize the subscriber quite badly. Where prices have been agreed in advance for several years, this has major benefits for both subscriber and publisher. Both are able to budget more accurately in the few years ahead. Time is also saved, as negotiations will not need to be carried out every year. The downside for the subscriber is that some flexibility in choice is lost should a new product come on the market. Clauses should be put in the contract that this renewal guarantee is subject to there being no major change in content.

Shortening the subscription term

A publisher will really know that things are tight financially if this suggestion is put forward for any reason other than to tie up a subscription with others by the same publisher. It may be that time is needed to verify if the product is highly regarded, and so there may be a suggestion that the product is only renewed for a period of several months in the first instance. Many publishers are flexible about the period of subscription, but some may need a lot of persuasion to do renewals shorter than a year. One good argument is that if the subscription term is not shortened to deal with a temporary budget problem, then the product will not be renewed at all. Then 'out of sight, out of mind . . .' means that the product may not be renewed in full in future years.

The financial year of the subscribing organization needs to be taken into account in this scenario. For example, shortening the subscription term to six months could be a temporary measure to pay less in the current financial year, but if renewing for a full term in the next financial year, then the price comparison will really stand out.

Price cap in future years

Obtaining a price cap is hedging one's bets. It does not tie the subscriber in and does not guarantee a renewal, but it gives a guideline for the future. This is especially useful where a publisher insists on a high price rise in the forthcoming year. This can be offset by zero or small increases in the next few years. A price cap can either be referred to as a figure or as a percentage increase on the current subscription price.

Price guideline

The converse to the price cap is also possible where a zero or small price increase has been negotiated for the next renewal, but is accompanied by warnings of larger rises to come. For example, the publisher might agree the masterfully negotiated small price increase, but give a price guideline for future years. The intention may be to increase in large, but manageable, steps to a price that reflects what the publisher considers the subscriber ought to be paying. This quite often happens after an organization comes out of a 'honeymoon' period with a product. It might be the result of a trial or using a product as a beta version.

Payment frequency

The majority of subscriptions are paid annually. For expensive subscriptions, paying in a different way can make a huge difference to the cash flow of both publisher and subscriber. For small start-up publishers with a new product, having an annual payment up front is quite attractive and may not be problematic to the large subscriber.

Where monthly payment is the norm, then asking for a discount if the subscription is paid up front may be of benefit. This could be an example of a 'win–win' situation for both subscriber and publisher.

If payments are made monthly, this needs to be taken into account when generating budgets for future years. For example, where a product was £6000 in one year and £6250 in the next year, depending on when the financial year of the organization falls, six payments may be at the old price and six at the new price, meaning the price of the product in that financial year is actually £6125.

Service level

Service level agreements (SLA) may be made or contract terms amended if it is deemed important and of value to the subscriber. The product will be less valuable if searches cannot be carried out, either because the database fails to work or where some users need the assistance of a helpdesk that is closed at certain times.

Publicity

A publisher may put a value on being able to tell the rest of the world that you are a subscriber to their product. This is especially valuable to new publishers. Each organization will have its own policy about whether information about what they subscribe to can be readily divulged. In some instances organizations may have a problem about being openly associated with a particular product, as this could be seen as endorsement and open them up to liability or ridicule if the product fails. Where there is no such problem, agreeing to the release of a press release or the organization's name appearing on a list of subscribers may encourage the publisher to look more favourably on other aspects of the subscription that are being sought.

Recommendation or introduction

Many services and products around the world get new customers through the recommendation of others – a cheap and valuable mechanism to the publisher. The informal passing on of a personal experience concerning a particular database is not something that the publishers can control. What can be done, however, is where a subscribing organization is part of a wider network, for instance a professional association which has affiliations or equivalents around the world, they might offer to write to the affiliated organizations mentioning how useful they find the particular product.

If someone writes letters of recommendation for all their products, then their recommendation ceases to help other organizations decide what is truly valuable. Therefore this is one option that should be used sparingly, and any letter should be worded carefully so as not to appear to endorse the product in a formal way.

Extended free trials

Trials can be more hard work than they are worth (see Chapter 1, p. 3). However, having access to a product, even temporarily, may have value to an organization. The length of an extended free trial may be as much as six months.

Subscribers should be cautious of accepting extended free trials in case it actually results in them paying more, rather than just getting more. There are three main types of extended free trial. The first is with an intention to buy. This is where there may be no money in a current budget but there are high expectations that the product will be well received by end-users. A publisher may make the judgement that an extended trial will only help to confirm how important the product is and will ensure a greater likelihood of them getting a deal. The second scenario is where a subscriber has one product and sees some small value in another, unrelated product. Having an extended free trial may be one way of sweetening a negotiation. The final example is where a publisher is bringing out a new product, and the product is in its testing phase. The publisher can get genuine feedback by allowing access to the product on a trial basis. Publishers often pay for feedback through market research and testing panels, so this certainly has value to the publisher. The subscriber has to balance up the amount of time they have to do this, the likelihood of having to subscribe once the trial is over, and what the publisher is offering in return, other than just access to a trial product.

Product enhancement

A decision may be made by a subscriber to add conditions to their contract or payment terms with regard to how the product develops. The sort of feature that may be of value or interest to an organization include:

- interface improvement
- search improvement
- more depth of content
- more breadth of content
- better access, such as IP authentication.

Product integration

Some subscribing organizations operate single-search functions or an alerting service that pulls from a variety of sources. Many publishers charge for their development time when having to work with a new product or software company. Therefore, this is a good area for negotiation if this sort of work is desirable. If a publisher does not charge for this work or they have previously demonstrated expertise in this area even at a cost to the subscriber, it may well be a bargaining tool that they can play to their advantage if they know that the choice is between their product and another one.

Sponsorship

Subscribing organizations and publishers may choose to advertise or promote themselves in a number of ways. Of relevance here are those where it has an effect on the relationship between publisher and purchaser (see Figure 3.5).

Sponsorship by the subscriber	Sponsorship by the publisher
• Writing content for journals and online resources • Sponsoring a page or subject on a particular online database • Co-sponsoring an event such as a training day or a conference	• Contributing funds or equipment to a particular department of an educational establishment • Co-sponsoring an event such as a training day or a conference • Sponsoring an event such as the AGM of a professional association of librarians

Figure 3.5   Sponsorship and the publisher—purchaser relationship

Being aware of these issues in the negotiation phase and whether they either exist or could be developed may make a proposition attractive to both publisher and organization alike.

Gifts

Many publishers give out chocolates at Christmas, and being a chocoholic, the author believes this practice should be encouraged. However, there is a fine line between a few chocolates, mints and mouse mats and more generous offerings of city-break weekends and a case of vintage wines. A negotiation should always be about the product and how it is used. A situation should not exist where the subscriber feels under an obligation due to an extravagant gift. Some organizations also have policies about accepting gifts, especially government departments, where they either have to be declared to a specific ombudsman or simply rejected, however small the gift.

David and Goliath — coping with the powerful

Larger subscribers or consortia generally have more bargaining power. It is not unusual for an information professional who works for a relatively small organization to sigh wistfully when they overhear at a conference how their counterpart in a larger organization managed to make massive savings on a particular product. The jealous information professional will know too well that the other organization is on the publisher's 'A list' and that their organization is small fry and hardly on the radar of the publisher.

How, though, does one tackle a negotiation where the other side is supremely more powerful? The party in the weaker position will have to focus on two main objectives. Their first is to protect themselves from making an agreement that is not acceptable. No one side should feel bullied into anything. The second objective is to make the most of what they do have in order to achieve as close to their aims as possible. Again, this means detailed analysis, this time at the preparation stage, to ensure there is adequate information about the product, how it is used and how valuable it is.

There are several strong arguments you can use.

The argument of principle

It is worth reminding the more powerful side that the basis of the negotiation is one of principle and fairness and not self-serving interest and power games.

Value argument

How the product contributes to the organization's success differs from organization to organization, and therefore a pricing or contract structure suitable to a larger organization does not apply for the smaller organization.

A thoroughly thought-through BATNA

The weaker party will have to have a stronger, more thoroughly explored BATNA. How far this BATNA is divulged to the other side is up to the negotiator. Explaining to the other side what would happen if no agreement were made can focus their attention. It is also worth considering what the stronger side's BATNA might be as this will give you an indication of how effective your arguments might be.

For a small or niche publisher dealing with a large consortium, a statement about the future of the product may remind some negotiators that it is not unheard of for products to cease to be available due to their non-profitability. However, this tack is a dangerous one as it could remind an organization about the vulnerability of dealing with a small company or start-up.

Respect me for at least trying

If you do not try to gain a better deal, then you will never know what might have been achieved.

Giving some ground helps to maintain a good relationship

The negotiator may not always stay with the small organization. They may end up negotiating at a larger firm and would look more kindly on a publisher who treats their subscribers equally. Similarly, the subscribing or publishing organization may not always remain in the weaker position – it may merge or grow.

Many smaller subscriber organizations feel that if they chose not to subscribe the publisher would not miss them or their money. However, it may be that the publisher's revenues for this product come mainly from small organizations. The publisher may therefore be concerned about any single organization ceasing to subscribe in case it indicates a trend that the product is not essential.

Smaller organizations can also increase their 'fighting weight' by assigning the negotiation to an agent or a consortium, or by belonging to a user group that involves large and small subscribers alike. However, it is sad reality that in many instances where there is a successful agreement between unequals, for the weaker player the terms are also more likely to be closer to their WAP than their MFP.

Examples of the sort of language that a weaker side might use include the following:

- What is the principle behind the proposed price rise?
- Our concern is one of fairness.
- If you are not prepared to meet us at least part way, then, although we really like your product, we will seriously have to consider whether we are able to continue our subscription.
- The value of this product to our organization is different from that of a larger organization.

What if they refuse to negotiate?

As mentioned before, a negotiation is about the movement of all involved to achieve a mutually acceptable outcome. If one side refuses to move, or if one side is having to make all the concessions, then it is not negotiation. Some tactics that can be tried to jump start the other side into a frame of mind where they might negotiate include the following:

- Ask them why they cannot negotiate:
  - They may have the wrong impression about what is expected from the negotiation and feel that there is no point in attempting the process. If you ask what the sticking point is, this may reveal something that can be worked around or upon. For example, they may say that they know the ability to disseminate information electronically to third parties is a deal-breaker for you, but that similar enquiries from other subscribers in the past have revealed that this is not an option they can offer; however, you may be able to explain that dissemination in hard copy is something you need to be able to do, and to ask whether there is room for movement on that option.
  - Alternatively, this may reveal that they do not have the authority to negotiate; an option here is to locate an appropriate person in the organization able to do so.
  - The worst scenario is that they make it very clear that it is an active decision not to negotiate. In this instance you can only appeal to their sense of fair play and point out that you are willing to play your part in a negotiation.

- Focus on the reasons *why* a negotiation is required, and take the emphasis away from their immovable position.
- Invite them to come up with some suggestions for solving the problem.
- Remind them that you are prepared to make concessions provided they can do the same for you.
- Use an 'If . . . then . . .' suggestion. For example, '*If* you are prepared to look at amending the contract terms, *then* I might be able to meet your asking price'.
- Give them a limited choice rather an open-ended question. For example, 'Which day is best to discuss this, Tuesday or Thursday?'
- Consider involving a third party such as an agent or arbitrator.

If you can identify the reason why they will not negotiate, then there is a greater likelihood of being able to find a path that will then allow negotiation. Common reasons for not wishing to negotiate include:

- the belief that negotiation means giving in – assure them that you are prepared to make compromises.
- anger due to previous experiences – either let them deal with another person or assure them that this time it is different.
- distrust or uncertainty – it is hard to negotiate when someone does not believe what the other person is saying. This experience may be based either on the experience of broken promises or not knowing the person well enough to judge their reliability. To get past this distrust the negotiation has to be very open and clear. If new people are involved, a preliminary 'get to know you' meeting can reap huge benefits by reassuring both sides.
- anger or disbelief due to initial reaction – a subscriber or publisher may be angry at what seems an unreasonable request and think that there is no point in negotiating as the starting point is so very far away from where they want to be. Invite them to state what would be more to their liking.

Summary

It takes two or more to negotiate and negotiation is far more than just words or positions. It is about developing and maintaining a good working relationship that provides the solid platform for a successful negotiation. Negotiation is about effective communication and we have explored the various methods that might be used. Examples of the sort of language that can be used at each stage of the negotiation are given, but the best language is that which the negotiator feels most comfortable with. Preparation is the cornerstone in our negotiation (see Chapter 1). The various aspects of an online subscription that can form the basis of negotiation have been discussed, as well as how to deal with the reluctant negotiator and the powerful one.

References

1   Fisher, R. and Ury, R. (1999) *Getting to Yes: negotiating an agreement without giving in*, 2nd edn, London, Random House, 41.

2   International Coalition of Library Consortia, www.library.yale.edu/consortia/statementsanddocuments.html [accessed August 2005].

3   CHEST Collections policy, www.eduserv.org.uk/chest/collections-policy.html [last updated 9 December 2003].

4   Negotiation Matrix, Michael Taylor Associates, Management Consultants, The Oast House, Horsegrove Farm, Rotherfield, East Sussex TN6 3LU, 2003.

5   John Ruskin, cited in Honomichl, J., A Price that's Too Good to be Good Usually Is, *Marketing News*, 4 February, 1991, 17.

6   McClelland, D.C. (1975) *Power: the inner experience*, New York, Irvington Press.

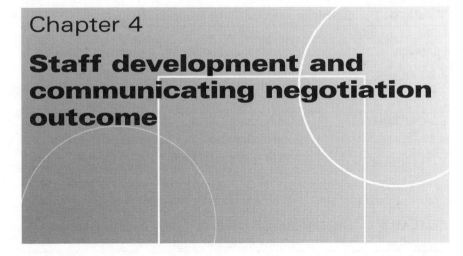

Chapter 4

Staff development and communicating negotiation outcome

This chapter is more relevant to the larger organization than to the sole trader or small organization. It aims to show how negotiation can play a key role in the continuing professional development of staff and ensure that the negotiator keeps a high profile within the firm. It also covers what to do once the negotiation has finished, who to keep informed and what information to record.

Staff development

As we have seen in previous chapters there are many skills involved in the negotiation process. As most managers know, it is good both to draw on existing skills and to encourage fledgling or new skills to ensure a well rounded team. Many people will be familiar with the concepts of Dr Meredith Belbin, who researched for many years what made a successful team. He identified the key roles that contributed to a successful team:[1]

- action-oriented roles – Shaper, Implementer and Completer Finisher
- people-oriented roles – Co-ordinator, Teamworker and Resource Investigator
- cerebral roles – Plant, Monitor Evaluator and Specialist

Table 4.1   Belbin's key roles in successful teams

Belbin Team role type	Contributions	Allowable weaknesses
PLANT	Creative, **imaginative**, unorthodox. **Solves difficult problems**.	Ignores incidentals. Too preoccupied to communicate effectively.
CO-ORDINATOR	Mature, **confident, a good chairperson**. **Clarifies goals**, promotes decision-making, delegates well.	Can often be seen as manipulative. Off-loads personal work.
MONITOR EVALUATOR	Sober, strategic and discerning. **Sees all options, judges accurately**.	Lacks drive and ability to inspire others.
IMPLEMENTER	Disciplined, reliable, conservative and efficient. **Turns ideas into practical actions**.	Somewhat inflexible. Slow to respond to new possibilities.
COMPLETER FINISHER	Painstaking, **conscientious**, anxious. **Searches out errors and omissions**, delivers on time.	Inclined to worry unduly. Reluctant to delegate.
RESOURCE INVESTIGATOR	Extrovert, **enthusiastic**, **communicative**. **Explores opportunities**, develops contacts.	Over-optimistic. Loses interest once initial enthusiasm has passed.
SHAPER	Challenging, dynamic, thrives on pressure. **The drive and courage to overcome obstacles**.	Prone to provocation. Offends people's feelings.
TEAMWORKER	**Co-operative**, mild, **perceptive, diplomatic**. **Listens**, builds, **averts friction**.	Indecisive in crunch situations.
SPECIALIST	Single-minded, self-starting, dedicated. **Provides knowledge and skills** in rare supply.	Contributes only on a narrow front. Dwells on technicalities.

Highlighted in Table 4.1 are the types of characteristic that you might find in a negotiator. These characteristics exist in many key roles that are needed in a team. According to Belbin, we usually find a role in which we are most comfortable, but we also have a 'back-up' role that we end up slotting into should this role be lacking in the team. Involving individuals in the negotiation process can help to develop additional skills for the benefit of individuals themselves and of the team.

It is essential that the key negotiator assigns the tasks clearly and puts them into context so that the individual has the chance to use their initiative should the opportunity arise. Tasks and roles that can be assigned include:

- research into the availability of alternative products
- management of trials of alternative or new products
- research into publicly available feedback on a product or selection of products
- conducting mini-interviews with end-users
- compiling a mini-survey for end-users
- being in charge of a particular group of communications, such as letters reserving the right to cancel
- reading the contract, maybe focusing on a particular section such as permissions and feeding back to the key negotiator any queries they have
- attending a meeting to provide information as an end-user.

An additional benefit of involving a varied number of team members includes there being a pool of those who know what goes on when a negotiation takes place. This ensures stability and knowledge within the team should there be leavers.

Statistics

Statistics can be a succinct way to show what has been achieved across a number of products or a number of years. Those in finance roles will understand statistics far better than the purpose of a product. Statistics are especially useful when having to deal with someone who has little or no knowledge of the products that are being sold or purchased. In order to compile useful statistics it is necessary to know the interests of the person to whom they will be presented. Given below are some examples of the sort of quick and simple statistics that can be compiled, ordered under the heading of the aspect which they demonstrate.

When a renewal is not on a like-for-like basis, the statistics need to be either pro-rated or a note appended to the figure to explain what might otherwise appear as a discrepancy.

Savings on initially quoted price

This is a statistic that demonstrates the negotiator's worth in monetary terms. The figure can be represented as either a total sum or a percentage. For example:

	FY06 price	FY07 quote	FY07 agreed price	Saving
Product Y	£ 2000	£ 2500	£ 2100	£400
Product Q	£ 7400	£ 8000	£ 7550	£450
Product X	£ 8000	£ 8400	£ 8400	£ 0
Product N	£14,550	£15,990	£15,000	£990

Total savings £1840

Increase on previous year's income/expenditure

This helps with budgetary planning and over a number of years can show a trend. It can be a poor indicator when there is constant variation in the level of subscription, for example where an organization is growing and prices go up to reflect the number of users. The figure can be represented as either a total sum or a percentage. The calculation for working out a percentage increase is:

$$\% \text{ change} = \frac{\text{new value} - \text{original value}}{\text{original value}} \times 100$$

	FY06 price	FY07 agreed price	Increase £	Increase %
Product Y	£ 2000	£ 2100	£100	5
Product Q	£ 7400	£ 7550	£150	2
Product X	£ 8000	£ 8400	£400	5
Product N	£14,550	£15,000	£450	3.1

Total increase £1100
Average % increase = 3.8%

This could also be demonstrated on a graph, which is especially useful over a number of years to see whether there are any trends, or if particular products stand out. If the products are anonymized, then the statistics can even be shown to the publisher and used for the purposes of a negotiation where an increase is vastly outside the organization's typical experience.

Usage levels

The level of usage can show the number of users or amount viewed per amount spent, and can be used by publishers and purchasers alike. This statistic is less likely to be used by the purchaser as one of their arguments in negotiation is often an attempt to break the link between number of users and prices. However, it may be a useful tool internally. As mentioned elsewhere, be cautious about using the amount viewed as a statistic as it can be argued that fewer pages viewed means that a search was a more efficient or a familiar one, or that the search interface was superior – all resulting in fewer pages viewed. In addition, the definition of a page view varies between publishers so it is more useful to compare year-on-year usage for the same product.

As per user

	FY06 price	Number of users	£ per user
Product Y	£ 2000	20	£ 100.00
Product Q	£ 7400	32	£ 231.25
Product X	£ 8000	5	£1600.00
Product N	£14,550	20	£ 727.50

As per page viewed

Product Y	Price	Number of viewed pages	£ per viewed page
FY06	£2000	8000	0.25
FY07	£2100	8750	0.24
FY08	£2250	8250	0.27

Even if someone has plenty of time to produce a huge amount of statistics, it is unlikely that large files of figures and graphs will be digested. Think about the audience and what facts they need. For a presentation, pull out only the essential figures. Decide what are the essential elements, extract the bare details and mention that there is back-up data should this need to be referred to.

Disseminating the results of negotiations

So the negotiation is all over, complete, the price agreed, the contract signed. If the deal was for a renewal, then much of the infrastructure around the product will be in place. People will be familiar with it, know how to use it and know what it contains. In many organizations most end-users do not realize that a momentous event has just taken place and you have saved the organization a lot of money and managed to get better contract terms too. It may be that this is what the information professional's job is all about, the seamless continuance of an end-user's access to a product. If this is the case, then telling end-users about the price of a product or even just that you are happy to announce that the product has been renewed this year is not necessary. However, if you have relied on some end-users for input into the decision-making process, then it may be courteous to inform them of the outcome in a brief way.

Consideration needs to be given to how much is communicated about savings or spending in general in case the wrong impression is made. Some insecure members of staff may see a lot of well advertised savings on online subscriptions as the result of pressure from the 'powers that be' and that the organization is financially unstable, whereas wild spending can also be questioned.

If a subscription is a new one, then more work needs to be done. Usually a trial will have shown that the product is compatible with other systems, but more work may need to be carried out, for example a wider roll-out of a particular piece of software that allows certain documents to be viewed. The key tasks are:

- to check that the system will work on all end-users' computers or general-access machines
- to sort out login or silent authentication issues with both the publisher and internal IT systems
- to verify a convenient start date with the publisher
- to make a convenient access point to the product for end-users, for example via a desktop icon, a catalogue entry or an internet favourite
- to arrange for a demonstration or training for end-users
- to integrate the product with other aspects of the organization, ranging from handouts to catalogues to search engines.

Recording the outcome of the negotiation

As mentioned in Chapter 1 on 'Preparation', the first stage in any negotiation is to refer to the deal that was made the previous year. Recording the outcome of a negotiation is therefore essential. The following information needs to be kept:

- figures, ranging from the price originally quoted to the final price agreed
- who was involved in the negotiation on both sides
- any amendments to the contract, in the format of either a highlighted contract or bullet points in a document

- any indication made at that negotiation of the direction of future negotiations
- any undertakings made by either side, such as providing feedback or improving the interface
- dates, such as when to review the subscription, when the subscription expires, and if there is a notification period.

Summary

Negotiation is recognized as just one part of the role of either publisher or information professional. It offers opportunities to develop individuals and teams. If a confident negotiator can mentor a junior then this experience cascades through the industry, resulting in ever more positive negotiations. How the achievements are recorded or communicated depends upon the needs of those involved, and, as with many jobs, a little or a lot can be done, depending on the resources available. If only one thing is recorded about a particular negotiation, this will still add to the body of experience; every lesson learned will make the next negotiation even better.

Reference

1　Belbin team roles, www.belbin.com/belbin-team-roles.htm (reproduced with kind permission from Jo Keeler of Belbin Associates).

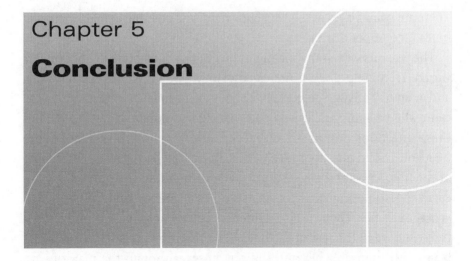

Chapter 5

Conclusion

Negotiating Licences for Digital Resources has been written as a practical guide on to how to get the best deal for online subscriptions. The processes outlined in this book can be applied to a wide range of electronic subscriptions, ranging from e-journals to multi-modular databases. There are practical tips and guidance on what to focus upon during the process of the negotiation and, most importantly, what preparation is needed to ensure you gather the necessary amount of information to achieve the best outcome. The timing of this advance preparation is one of the skills that enables the negotiator to feel in control. Appendix 2 outlines the key considerations in the timing process and offers a sample timeline to help your planning and preparation. The intention throughout this book has been to move logically from understanding your organization's needs, to making the contract more understandable, through to the actual negotiation process in written or face-to-face scenarios.

A lot of what has been written may already be part of your professional experience, but you may not have realized how much you already knew. A book cannot have all the answers, of course, but hopefully there are at least some starting points here. As you get involved in more negotiations, make a note of what works (and what does not work!) and add to this book.

There are some pages at the very end where it is possible to make personal notes (see Appendix 3).

The reasons why someone might buy or read this book are not hugely varied. They are probably interested in improving their negotiation skills and in finding answers to questions about the negotiation process and what can really be achieved. It is hoped that this book has addressed a lot of these questions but, as an additional aid, Appendix 1 contains some frequently asked questions (FAQs) that are designed to draw together some of the tips, ideas and suggestions made throughout the book. They are easily digestible and can be used as a quick reference guide where speed is of the essence. They are also written in a different format to complement the structure of the rest of the book. The selection consists of questions from both the publisher and the purchaser, although the majority are purchaser questions as it is often the purchaser who is the least experienced negotiatior.

It is hoped that a wide range of professionals will find this book useful, from information professionals, knowledge managers, online resource buyers and e-journal agents to vendors of online resources and procurement officers. These professionals are cross-sectoral, ranging from academic librarians to in-house knowledge managers and sales representatives. Negotiation is a topic that is universal in both sector and geography. Each person involved in discussing a deal will have different levels of knowledge about the product, their own and their counterpart's organization, their financial goals and how it all fits into providing a value-for-money online product.

Negotiating is something that always offers new learning opportunities. Each negotiation is different, but many of the same ideas and concepts can be applied across varied situations. Making a note of what works in a particularly difficult negotiation will remind you how much has actually been achieved as well as being a reference tool for future negotiations.

Any person can carry out a negotiation, but those with certain skills, such as visual and listening skills, the ability to see different perspectives, confidence, determination and imagination, will have an easier time. The tips in this book aim to develop some of these skills, through building confidence (with thoughtful preparation) and imagination (by providing suggestions). A lot of importance has been placed on adequate preparation – gathering information prior to the exchange of words stage in a negotiation.

Negotiation is very frequently worth the time and effort. It is about moving towards a mutually satisfactory outcome. Negotiation is about thinking how to achieve goals while respecting that others have their goals too. Negotiation is about not being too scared to say what you think, about not being too worried about the reaction of others to your suggestions or points of view. Negotiation is not about getting everything you want, but rather about getting key aspects of what you want. Occasionally the outcome is not what was sought, but this has to be balanced with the times when success is achieved.

As the author Marcia Martin says:

> What I point out to people is that it's silly to be afraid that you're not going to get what you want if you ask. Because you are already not getting what you want. They always laugh about that because they realize it's so true. Without asking you already have failed, you already have nothing. What are you afraid of? You're afraid of getting what you already have! It's ridiculous! Who cares if you don't get it when you ask for it, because, before you ask for it, you don't have it anyway. So there's really nothing to be afraid of.[1]

Or as Mahatma Gandhi more succinctly put it: 'If you don't ask, you don't get'.

Reference

1   Cited in Canfield, J. and Hansen, M. V. (1995) *The Aladdin Factor*, New York, Berkley Publishing.

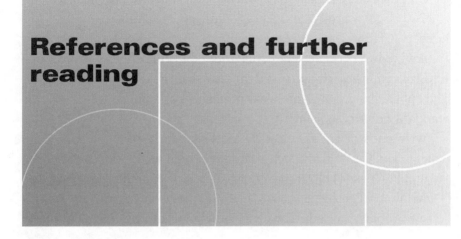

References and further reading

Books

Canfield, J. and Hansen, M. V. (1999) *The Aladdin Factor*, New York Berkley Publishing.

Fisher, R. and Ury, W. (1999) *Getting to Yes: negotiating an agreement without giving in*, 2nd edn, London, Random House.

Forsyth, P. (2000) *The Negotiator's Pocketbook*, London, Management Pocketbooks.

McClelland, D. C. (1975) *Power: the inner experience*, New York, Irvington Press.

Quillam, S. (2004) *Body Language*, London, Carlton Books.

Ury, W. (1991) *Getting Past No: negotiating with difficult people*, London, Random House.

Wainright, G. R. (2003) *Body Language*, London, Hodder & Stoughton.

Websites

Belbin team roles, www.belbin.com/belbin-team-roles.htm.

CHEST Collections policy, www.eduserv.org.uk/chest/collections-policy.html [last updated 9 December 2003].

COUNTER Code of Practice for Journals and Databases (published April 2005), www.projectcounter.org/code_practice.html.

Eduserv/CHEST Datasets Agreements, www.eduserv.org.uk/chest/datasets/table-index.html.

JISC collections, www.jisc.ac.uk/collbrowse.html.

The Publishers' Association, www.publishers.org.uk.

Standard Eduserv agreement, www.eduserv.org.uk/chest/datasets-agreement.rtf.

Statement of Current Perspective and Preferred Practices for the Selection and Purchase of Electronic Information by the International Coalition of Library Consortia, www.library.yale.edu/consortia/statementsanddocuments.html.

Appendix 1
Frequently asked questions

The questions that follow are ones that I have come across either during training sessions, informal chats, or in response to real negotiation situations. The answers are suggestions; there may well be alternatives in either approach or solution.

SQ = Subscriber question
PQ = Publisher question

SQ: **What if the publisher, after numerous attempts, won't negotiate on the price?**

A: Use the following checklist:

- What are your WAP and your BATNA?
- Are the publishers prepared to make concessions on aspects other than the price?
- If desirable, can a deal be done for future years to mitigate the price increase in the long term?
- If the publisher will not negotiate on price or other terms, point out to them that without some movement on their part this is not negotiation and that you are

prepared to offer concessions. Use the ideas about how to get someone to the negotiation table (see Chapter 3, pp.115–17).

- Consider where complaints about unfair pricing can be taken, such as an industry body or professional association.
- Consider whether the resource can be negotiated by a consortium.

PQ: **Why can't you just pay what we ask without causing a fuss? It would make life so much easier.**

A: Subscribers are prepared to pay what is asked without a fuss when the price and terms are fair.

SQ: **We are small fry, why would the publisher bother negotiating with us?**

A: Because you ask. Refer to the section on David and Goliath situations in Chapter 3 (pp. 113–15).

SQ: **What are our chances of getting terms in a contract changed?**

A: Getting contract terms changed depends on a number of factors. These include:

- whether the publisher is the owner or just the re-seller of the content. In the latter situation, where the publisher might be an aggregator, they will probably have separately negotiated terms with a large number of content owners and changing some contract terms may therefore be a logistical nightmare for the publisher.
- whether the contract is based on a winning tender where specific contract terms were specified.
- whether a consortium is negotiating the contract terms.

- how the publisher draws up its contracts. For example, have they their own in-house legal team or did they contract out the writing of their contracts?

Bear in mind that seeking clarification does not mean the contract has to be changed: often an e-mail clarifying the point is sufficient.

SQ & PQ: How do I know I've got the best deal for my renewal?

A: It is one that both sides are happy with so future renewals are also sustainable. Where negotiation has taken place, both sides will have made some concessions and the price and terms compare favourably with previous years. Usually the time to stop pressing is once the proposal has been referred to a higher authority and approval gained. Doing that on more than one occasion is not usually acceptable.

SQ: I want to start, rather than renew, a subscription. How do I know whether I am paying a fair price?

A: It is important to get the first negotiation right as this is often the reference point for future negotiations. Work out:

- what value the product has to the organization
- whether it is replacing something else that has a value
- whether there is a competitor product on the market that has a price
- whether the product's price is published either on the publisher's website or on a consortium's website.

PQ: I am a small start-up online publishing company. How do I price a subscription fairly? Costs are quite heavy in the beginning but as I get more subscribers my relative costs will go down.

A: Investment in a product over the long term needs to be taken into account. Talk to your industry association (e.g. in the UK The Publishers' Association).[1] They will have statistics and guidance to offer. Membership of the PA in the UK even entitles you to one hour with a financial consultant. The usual model is to price with an estimate based on the cost and the number of subscribers in the long term. However, pricing does not always have to be one that starts low and goes up. To get long-term loyalty one option is to be very open with potential subscribers and let them know that when you get more subscribers prices will actually start to go down.

SQ: **I don't have time to negotiate all my online subscriptions, so how do I prioritize?**

A: This is up to each organization but is usually a combination of how much the product costs, how important that product is to the organization and whether there is a large increase in price or major change to the terms and conditions.

SQ & PQ: **I don't have time to be negotiating every year, but I always want to get the best deal. What do I do?**

A: Consider multi-year deals or price caps. The latter won't do away with the negotiation but will make the next year's negotiation that much swifter as much of the work will already have been done.

SQ: **I have an agent who deals with the negotiation of all or some of my online subscriptions, but how do I know I am getting the best deal?**

A: Look at the agreement between your agent and yourself. Is there an incentive for your agent to negotiate the price down? Also, by the time you've communicated to your agent what you need in the contract, would it have been easier for you to have done this directly? Ask your agent if they benefit from bulk-buying discounts that they can pass on to you.

SQ: **My industry/sector seems particularly bad for prices. Is there anything I can do?**

A: As you have the same industry in common, consider whether a consortium-negotiated licence is an option. See whether your professional body can do a comparison of price rises with their own and another sector, as this could lend weight to any arguments in negotiations.

SQ: **My representative is really poor at dealing with issues throughout the year but near negotiation time is miraculously able to pay attention to my requests. What can I do?**

A: Consider whether you need a separate service level agreement. Other options include making the agreement conditional on certain issues being dealt with within a specific timeframe over the course of the contract. Also keep examples of poor responses as these are ammunition at negotiation time. If the problem persists and the publisher is big enough, you can explore whether a different representative would be better for you.

SQ: **The pricing structures offered by the publisher just do not match our needs. What can I do?**

A: Discuss with the publisher why the pricing structures offered do not work for you. Use the arguments in Chapter 3 about the deal needing to be 'fair' (pp.73-9). Explain that it is not a price issue but a transparency issue – for internal justification you need to have a pricing structure that can apply to your organization. Investigate whether the content is sold by someone else who does have a structure that you can work with.

PQ: **How do I make the deal attractive to the subscriber?**

A: It all depends on the subscriber and what their priorities are. They may not value additional content, free trials or integration into other software. Focus on their priorities and the deal will be more attractive. Effective communication is the route to achieving this.

Reference

1   See The Publishers' Association website for membership benefits: www.publishers.org.uk.

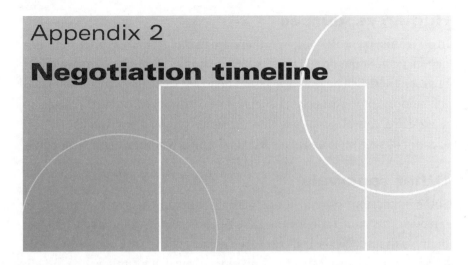

Appendix 2
Negotiation timeline

When an organization decides to carry out a particular stage of the negotiation process will depend on a number of factors. These are explored below.

Contract length

Typically a contract is for one year, but more commonly longer contracts are agreed, especially by consortia. Short contract periods of six months or less often make the process feel like a treadmill. A contract of several years will allow for more flexibility and give the negotiators some time to build up a relationship other than one based on contract terms and prices.

Cancellation terms

The cancellation terms in a contract may determine by when a subscribing organization needs to be having serious discussions with the publisher so that they are not in a position where they are obliged to renew, even if ceasing to subscribe is not seen as an option. As mentioned in Chapter 1 on 'Preparation', when there is a specification in the contract about when the subscriber has to notify the publisher if they wish to cancel, one way around this is to write a letter reserving the right to cancel.

Human resources

In all teams, regardless of size, there are many pressures other than just negotiation. Some organizations have teams dedicated to procurement, but even these will have issues of staff holidays, sickness or maternity leave. It is important to realize that such events cannot always be predicted so make sure you allow a 'cushion' of time, say of a few weeks, to take account of such staffing issues when planning your negotiation schedule.

Other renewals

Some subscriber organizations actually like all their subscriptions to renew at the same time for the sake of consistency, some like to stagger them so that renewals and costs are spread out over the course of a year. Where there are other products due for renewal at a similar time, one or more renewal discussions may need to be bought forward.

Budgetary data

Organizations manage their budgets in different ways, ranging from guestimates to figures based on actual negotiated prices. Other examples of budgetary planning include raising the amount by an agreed percentage or sum of money. If there is a need for a budget to be accurate and as close to what is going to be spent as possible, then negotiations may well need to be carried out quite far in advance. For example, if the financial year is from January to December, the budget may have to be submitted by the Head of Information by the end of July. Figures will therefore need to be coming in during the first half of the year. Where a subscription to a product runs from the beginning of July to the end of June, this will mean getting a price a year or more ahead of the actual renewal date.

If the person involved in the negotiation is not the one to recommend what is needed in forthcoming years for the budget, then their major constraint will be knowing what has been set. This may encourage some negotiations to take place rather too close to their renewal date for comfort. If there is a large number of such renewals, then issues about the contract terms can be discussed first, with some movement made on the issue of price based on what is felt fair, what trends there have been in the past, and any hints given about the extent of the budget. The final tweaks to the negotiation can then take place closer to the renewal time.

Sales representatives may have been set goals and targets. If these goals and targets are specific to each contract, then there is less room for manoeuvre. However, if the goals are spread across a period of time, then there may be more flexibility in what they can offer or compromise upon.

Busy times of the year

Some sectors or industries have certain times of the year where they are exceptionally busy. For example, in universities the end of September and beginning of October are very busy due to the start of the academic year. For publishers, December is often a busy time of the year as many subscriptions are ending or up for renewal at this time of year. The solution is either to try not to have products renewing at this time or to be aware of these 'bottlenecks' and to bring the discussions forward.

Nice to do

There are some tasks that might only need to be carried out every few years, depending on the length of the contract or type of task. For example, carrying out a survey of users' opinions every year would soon annoy the users and cease to yield useful results. Other similar tasks that might be carried out periodically include research into competitor products and getting usage statistics.

An example of what might take place on a typical one-year cycle contract is given overleaf.

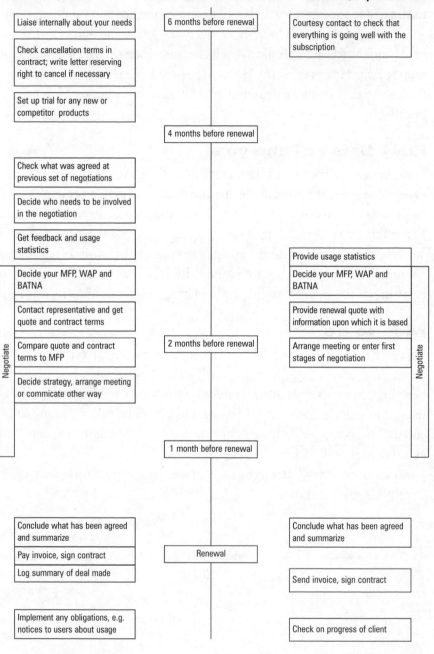

Figure A2.1 A typical one-year cycle contract

Appendix 3

Personal negotiation experience

Successful arguments or tactics

Argument	Reason why it worked

Unsuccessful arguments or tactics

Argument	Reason why it failed

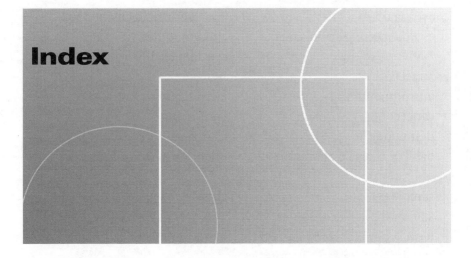

Index